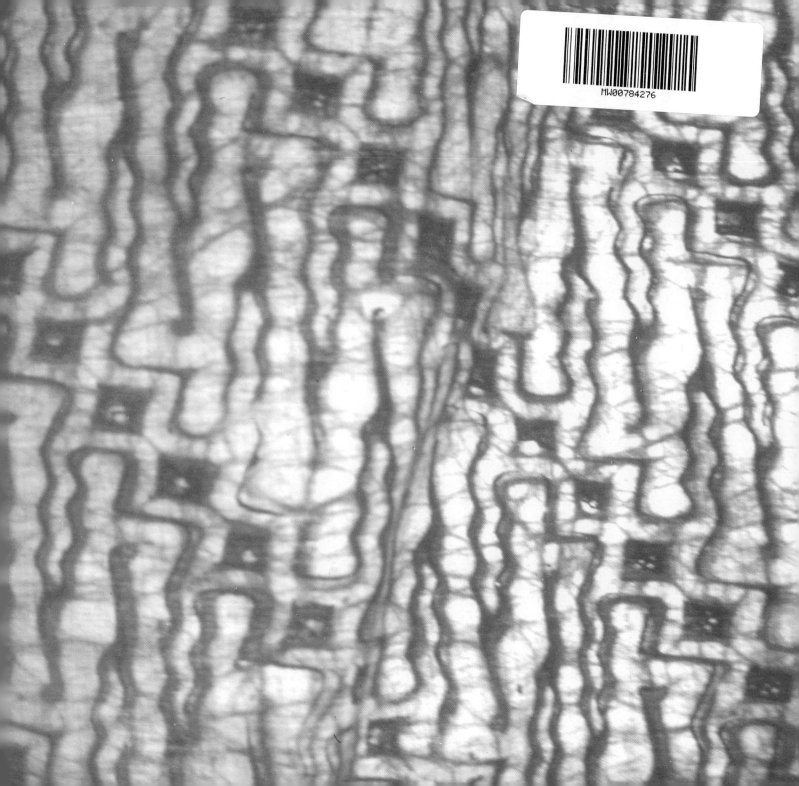

Indonesian Street Food Secrets

A Culinary Travel Odyssey

Keith Ruskin Miller

Indonesian Street Food Secrets

1st edition

Published by

Hawkibinkler Press Ltd.
7725 N. Fowler St.
Portland, OR 97217, USA

Art and Photography

All of the images in this book are available for licensing.
Email: images@streetfoodsecrets.com
www.streetfoodsecrets.com

Published

June 2002

Text and photos © Hawkibinkler Press Ltd. 2002
Drawings © L. Don Miller, 1998

Printed in Indonesia by Pt. Indonesia Printer
Library of Congress Control Number 2002109801
ISBN 0 - 9721069 - 0 - 1

The drawings in this book were contributed by my father, L. Don Miller. His encouragement and love for travel never waned and this book is dedicated in his loving memory.

This project began as a Master's thesis to create a CD-ROM. In the intervening eight years the concept has gone from virtual to hard copy cookbook. Along the way many people contributed in ways impossible to quantify. Regrettably I have no records for the many Indonesians who assisted me during my first romp through their country. If it were not for their warmth and enthusiasm this project would never have crystalized. The germ of the idea and many hours of cranky development were endured by Jenny. Thank you for your patience and support and for your discrimination in finding the best places to eat. I also thank your family for introducing me to a variety of foods including some of the finest martabak in Bandung.

I spent a number of years back in the States mulling over the information gathered and building momentum. During that time I received help and guidance in San Diego from Greg Durbin who chaired my thesis committee and suggested I write this book. Bernie Dodge guided me through some of the finer points, and Mike Salomon, Rod Sheffield, Gar House and Michelle Warn were all generous with their encouragement.

In Portland, Oregon, I gained the momentum I needed to clear some final hurdles and return to Indonesia. Among those most instrumental were John Goldhammer who provided a mirror for my subconscious, John Ames who accompanied me on gastronomic hiking trips where ideas percolated, Karen Wilson who photographed some of my food in her studio, and her delightful mother Taj who became my close confidant. Steve Robbins coached me through some of the darkest hours and many others including Rhe Tah and David, Brian Bracelin, Bruce Brewer, Curt Cyr, Mike Davis, Mike Doss, Kirby Welch and all the men of Heartwood contributed immeasurably.

My mother, Martha Miller, inspired me to write, and spent many hours critiquing my work, always believing I would finish this book. Donna, Nate and Kamen all encouraged me to travel and to cook for them when I returned.

Back on the trail in Indonesia I encountered an amazing level of assistance and support. In Jakarta I thank Natalia for her knowledge and passion of the local food. In Bali, Dasak Nyoman was extremely generous with her recipes as was Pak Sunardi, Ibu Siti Baroroh, Pak Yamanto and Rini Astuti in Java. In Yogyakarta I received help from Wahyu Mukti Kusumaningtias as well as the staff of the Via Via Cafe, especially Desak Madé Ari Andayani.

More technical help came from Marc Schultz in Bangkok and Karen and Deniek Sukarya in Jakarta. Idaman D. Fahmy got me up to speed on printing issues. In Yogyakarta, drum scanning magic was contributed by A. Redyantoro at Primascan and color separations by Ortindo Imagesetter. Also thanks to Hendarmin Susilo and B. Sufeni S. at Gema Nada Pertiwi Pt. of Jakarta for providing the music that accompanies the CD-ROM (www.gnpmusic.co.id).

Lastly thanks to Imelda Riana for listening to me and enduring my final days of madness.

Clockwise from top:
1) Balinese kids,
2) lunch in Jepara, Java.
3) Yamanto family in Tempel, Java,
4) banana vendor in Cirebon, Java.

Keith Ruskin Miller has been cooking and creating multimedia content for the last 20 years. He financed his initial trips to Asia by consulting in video and multimedia design. He has traveled extensively both researching exotic food and working for a variety of clients including The Hong Kong Space Museum and The National Museum of Natural Science in Taichung, Taiwan. Keith currently resides part time in Java, Indonesia and part time in Portland, Oregon where he enjoys documenting World cuisines.

Contents

Clockwise from the top: 1) terraced rice fields in Central Bali, 2) the temple of Borobudur, 3) ancient Sanskrit text inscribed on a stone near Bukittinggi, Sumatra, 4) the steaming crater of gunung Bromo in East Java

Mangan Ora Mangan Ngumpul

Eat Or Not We Stay Together

In the South Indian Ocean, straddling the equator just south of the Philippines, and stretching from mainland Asia all the way to Papua New Guinea, there lies a vast archipelago of perhaps eighteen-thousand islands. Violent volcanic activity has encouraged these mountains to rise above the sea and provide niches for ecosystems diverging from dry and arid savannas to lush and tropical rain forests. Immense volcanic peaks preside over sapphire coral reefs and jagged coastal valleys where local populations are isolated even from their neighbors on the same island. Niches like these have preserved an ethnic diversity that accounts for over 700 distinct and living languages.

When the hominid Java man walked here 700,000 years ago he may have faced competition from other nomadic protohumans during an age before Java, Sumatra and Borneo broke away from the Asian continent and drifted into the sea. These early human inhabitants must have conducted experiments with the local vegetation; they probably ate everything in sight. Eventually they developed lore for incorporating indigenous seeds, grasses, leaves and roots into their foods. By the first millennium BC they were cultivating rice and domesticating animals.

The ensuing history of the archipelago is a story of continuous seasonings from the most advanced cultures of the day. The great seafaring powers that plied the seas between China and the Middle East found the archipelago smack in the middle of their trade routes. Not only was this a convenient port of call, but nature had granted these islands an exclusive concession in spices that were worth their weight in gold. As trade increased, foreigners came in ever-greater numbers and introduced strange religions and philosophies. Some of their practices involved novel ingredients and cooking techniques that were eventually adopted and transformed into something uniquely Indonesian.

Dwarapalas guard the temples of Plaosan near Prambanan in Central Java

By the Han Dynasty (206 BC – 220 AD), Chinese merchants were jabbering about soybeans and demonstrating how to cook noodles and tofu in a wok. Nowadays *mie goreng* (fried noodles) cooked in a *wajon* (wok) is one of the most common of Indonesian street foods, and *tahu* (tofu) is found in just about every *warung*. The locals also figured out how to maximize the protein potential of the soybean by mixing it with an obscure mold they found growing on hibiscus leaves. The result was the tempeh that is appreciated today by vegetarians worldwide.

Underground stairway to the Taman Sari (water castle) in Yogyakarta

Around the same time, but from the opposite direction, Indian traders arrived. They must have had more missionary zeal than their Chinese counterparts, because their model of a Hindu city state took hold on Sumatra and Java, and empires began to spread far and wide. The Indian pantheon of Gods and Goddesses was graciously invited to steep for awhile in the native animism, and to morph with an adapted flavor of Buddhism. In another cauldron, wondrous curries were embraced and enhanced to contain coconut milk and local spices. Stowaways on board ships from India included coriander, cumin, cucumbers, mangos, eggplants, and onions.

Not long after Islam swept through the Middle East, it began to take hold in the Islands, especially in the port cities. Missionaries accompanying Arab merchants advocated Islam as a casteless system with salvation for all. After curing for a time in the local Hindu-Buddhist animism, a unique hybrid of Islam took hold that has endured to the present day to find Indonesia the largest Moslem country in the World. During those early days, the mutton kebab was also pondered and eventually embellished to include a marinade of sweet and sour tamarind, and a topping of spicy peanut sauce.

Anxious to profit directly from the spice trade, Europeans managed to find their way to the region late in the fifteenth century. After getting lost for a spell in the new world, Portuguese and Spanish ships arrived first. While in the Americas, they "discovered" tomatoes, corn, peanuts, not-to-mention the transformational Eucharist,

Clockwise from top: 1) kids in Bukittinggi, Sumatra, 2) gamelan orchestra in Jakarta, 3) kecak dance troupe in Ubud, Bali

Street kids in Bogor, Java

the chili pepper. Apparently unaware of what they were instigating, they blithely handed the little capsicums over to the locals.

Dutch and English ships arrived next with superior naval power. The Dutch East India Company focused on the archipelago and the initial profits where enormous. However by 1799 woeful mismanagement lead to their bankruptcy. Not willing to give up such a bountiful string of pearls, the government of the Netherlands ponied up and transformed the entire archipelago into a vast colonial plantation. The locals were treated to the arrogance and hegemony that was fashionable at the time, but they did manage to pass some of this difficult period teasing intoxicating flavors from the carrots, cabbage, and cau-

liflower brought from Europe. They also corrupted European pastries into a mystical cult of sweet *kue*.

The Republic of Indonesia won its independence in 1949 and today the culinary horizons have never been brighter. Competition from American fast food joints has lead to some interesting street food hamburgers and KFC clones, but thankfully traditional Indonesian dishes are still in hot demand and readily available on every street corner. Regional diversity is overwhelming with dishes that change names and ingredients every 50 kilometers or so. Although you would need several lifetimes to sample them all, the brave explorer need only step out onto the sidewalk to encounter one of the world's greatest, albeit little-known cuisines.

*Clockwise
from top:
1) grandmother
and grandson
in Sumatra,
2) hanging
out in
Sulawesi,
3) Sumatran
lad,
4) selling
hicama in
Sumba
5) stone relief
at Borobudur*

15   Introduction

Rahasia

The disorientation and reorientation which comes with the initiation into any mystery is the most wonderful experience which it is possible to have.

-Henry Miller,
Tropic of Capricorn

June 5, 1996

The train rumbles and shakes as it drops out of the narrowing peninsula of southern Thailand and decelerates onto the jungle plains of Malaysia. Before it has rolled to a stop food hawkers are already on board, toting baskets full of unknown treats wrapped neatly in banana leaves. As I reach into my pockets wondering if my Thai baht is worth anything now, an earthy, round-faced woman stops beside me to inquire politely. I point to several of her organic little packages and listen intently as she speaks their names. Her speech is punctuated with a cadence, the signature of which is several wavelengths more exotic than the Thai, which had sounded quite exotic just last week. A few more food words are followed by some money words and we make our transaction.

The banana leaves are cool to my touch as I peel open the first to reveal a golden-brown wafer. It looks like a nut bar, but the smell and taste are wonderfully exotic and vaguely reminiscent of mushrooms. Inside

the second is a shiny mound of white rice covered with fried shallots and some tiny chili peppers. It smells fresh, almost floral, with a hint of coconut. The woman's words still linger in my mind: *tempe, nasi uduk, enak.* Her meaning seems so thoroughly enfolded into the textures, aromas, and flavors of these foods. What synaesthesia! So the world is constructed of language! Yet language is so completely inadequate for describing the mystery from which it springs. I can not understand these new words, however am I not what I eat? With a new language, and a new cuisine, have I not entered into a new reality? I sense the mystery of the logos looming closer, just out of reach. Is exotic cuisine the secret to reaching it?

"Hello mister, you like tempe-lah?" Apparently the man sitting across from me has been watching me this entire time with a huge grin on his face. He is an Indonesian, and he confides in me that although the two countries share a similar language, and although in his opinion Malaysia is a more developed country, the best food still comes from Indonesia. I ask him my inevitable question, "Is there much good street food there?" His eyes brighten at this and he chuckles. "Street food!" he says, "That is the king of street food mister! There are many! But you are not scared of spicy? I think Indonesian food is too spicy for your country."

Gado gado warung in Wonosobo, Java.

Introduction

my monkey brain. It was like a squeegee on my window of perception, leaving it clean and able to look upon the world with fresh eyes.

Two years later I arrived in Hong Kong resolved to explore this culinary-linguistic mystery at its source. I headed west across China and the Gobi Desert, then south through Tibet, Nepal and India. I learned all about "rubber time" making use of local transport to crawl from one check mark on the map to the next. How many times did I arrive hungry and torpid at some dusty road stop, only to find myself strangely energized by the vitality of the local culture and cuisine? It felt each time as if another layer of Western collective reality had dissolved between my ears.

Above: Nasi Gudeg and trimmings in Yogyakarta, Central Java

In a feeble attempt to show him my mantle I bite into my bird pepper. He doesn't seem to notice. As far as being the street food king goes, I have just spent a month eating my way through the Kingdom of Thailand, so I find that claim a little difficult to believe. But with the mystery so close at hand and Indonesia next on the itinerary, I am willing to give him the benefit of the doubt.

I have been stalking this dynamic between language and cuisine for nearly ten years. When I lived in Seattle I became enamored with the International District and all its various Asian restaurants. I often visited hole-in-the-wall joints just to eat in an atmosphere devoid of English. The synergy between strange foods and unfamiliar languages got my juices going, engaged my senses on multiple levels, and short-circuited

Late night fried rice in Bogor, East Java

Enjoying Es Campur (p. 115) in Toraja, Sulawesi

June 15

I have arrived in Sumatra today. I am not disappointed. There is street food everywhere.

July 10, 3 PM

I am listening to a growling conversation in my stomach as I gaze out the open window of a crowded bus headed for Malang on Eastern Java. While in Sumatra, I hooked up with an Aussie named Grant who shared a common interest in consuming bizarre street foods. Both of us are silent now, eager to deny the reality of this lumbering metal shell as it lurches along tormented by an ancient road. I can just barely shift my numb and contorted legs as I peer out at the occasional food stall, or kite-flying kid running along the road, or smooth-green papaya. My gaze stretches out over patches of rice paddy so green as to transport me momentarily out of this heat.

Hours later

A cool darkness has fallen. The bus pulls into a station and screeches to a halt. We all rise and ride a human wave down the aisle, out the narrow door, and several meters along the gravel pavement. I look up and find myself in the midst of a *pasar malam*; the night market that is located at the perimeters of the bus station. It is alive with activity.

Grant hoists his backpack and announces: "I'm bloody hungry mate! Reckon I'll have a look at some of that amazing *ayam goreng*!" He proceeds to make inquiries among a group of smiling men engulfed in a cloud of sweet kretek smoke. In addition to Aus-

Introduction

Presently, a quixotic scent catches my attention. It seems to emanate from behind a brightly painted banner that declares: *Opor Ayam Bukittinggi. Opor* is a kind of curry, *ayam* is chicken, and the last word is the name of a town I recently visited in Sumatra. *Bukittinggi* literally means high mountains, and the place is surrounded by picturesque volcanoes and brimming with delicious street food. Entering the little stall, I peer into a cauldron which seems to be the source of the mesmerizing fragrance billowing forth. "*Apa ini?*"

"*Ini opor enak!*" a tiny woman replies as she stirs the pot and reveals a velvety sauce that radiates a sunset shade of turmeric. "*Mau?*" she asks. "*Mau!*" I

Ayam Goreng (fried chicken, p. 103); always with rice and hot sambal (chili relish, p. 71)

tralian, Grant speaks excellent Indonesian, and he is not kidding about the ayam goreng. I'm freaking starving and the very thought of Indonesian fried chicken brings on visions of lovely drumsticks, marinated in tamarind and coconut milk, and fried to a golden crispiness the likes of which the Kentucky-fried Colonel might only dream.

As usual this market is serviced by a ramshackle assortment of food stalls. I wander along, responding in phrase-book Indonesian to the endless calls of "*hello mister,*" the final "r" of which is trilled with a dexterity that I cannot duplicate. Instead I say, "*apa ini?*" "What is this?" The vendors all respond guilelessly with the playful good nature that is so typical among Indonesians, and an eagerness to draw me into their warungs.

reply and she is promptly ladling out a modest serving across a bed of plump, steaming rice. As she sets the plate before me, the aromas of galingale, lemon grass, and coconut milk swirl upward and I have an odd sensation of deriving nourishment through the very pores of my skin. My appetite is enormous, but I restrain myself a moment longer and inspect the morsels with a fork and let the steam engulf me. In this moment, the chicken has become one with the *bumbu* (spice paste), and I take refuge in the dharma of curry.

As I polish off round two, I compliment the chef and ask her exactly what this delicacy consists of. She laughs and begins an elaborate chattering response. I nod my head pretending to understand her, but one word is repeated often enough to be unmistakable: *rahasia*. As my mind stretches to grasp the meaning of her words, my imagination provides a few missing details. I see myself running through a verdant jungle engaged in a quest for magical ingredients. I am a warrior chef, full of honor to hail from this mountainous kingdom of Bukittinggi. I alone know the alchemical formula for paying homage to the gods and safeguarding my family and my tribe. And I am proud to share in the honor, and the glory, and the opor ayam.

Back on planet Java, I notice the woman has finished talking and is standing there with a satisfied grin on her face. I gather my thoughts and rephrase my request, but it's no use. Conceding defeat, I order another plateful of the wicked-tasty stuff. Just then Grant wanders by munching from a bag of *rempeyek* (Indonesian peanut brittle), and wearing the satisfied look of a shoestring traveler. I wager him that if he can charm this woman out of her recipe, then I'll gladly treat him to a plate of the magic opor. He accepts my challenge and engages the woman in a lively dialog. She beams, shaking her head and repeating, "*Rahasia, mister, rahasia!*" A small crowd has gathered and they contribute with their teasing and laughter. Finally Grant turns to me and says, "oh it's a bloody secret mate! She's kept it a secret twenty-five years and reckons she's the only one round here that can make it; everyone comes round to see her!"

I grab a cigarette from Grant's shirt pocket. It crackles as it ignites and encourages further brooding. The hospitality of these people is so enormous. How could she withhold this ancient gem of culinary wisdom from me? After all my searching I deserve to know this. Am I not worthy of it?

Who am I kidding. I quit smoking two weeks ago and now I'm trying to look good in front of these people? Extinguishing the smoke I look up into the smiling eyes all around me and find it impossible to repress my own sheepish grin. I have been trying to quantify and transcribe something that cannot be reduced to words. Feeling humbled, yet strangely included in their world, I resolve to let another layer of my preconceived notions melt away. The secret is in the experience itself. Meanwhile I will simply absorb what I can of this great culinary tradition.

Opor Ayam Bukittinggi (p. 102) is one of the sublime pleasures of this world

Secrets of the Warung

Everywhere you look you see them: clustering at the perimeters of the *pasar malam* (night market), sprouting like mushrooms on sidewalks next to busy intersections, or lining the narrow footpaths between buildings. Indonesian street food is the ultimate fast food and it's ubiquitous. When you travel in Indonesia, you needn't miss out on good home cooking either. Loads of street food is prepared ahead of time in the cook's home and according to traditional family recipes.

Warung in Madura

Every morning they set to work, orchestrating flavors and textures as varied as the islands they hail from. Using all kinds of aromatic roots, leaves, and spices, delicious flavors are coaxed out of ordinary meats, vegetables, and rice. Bitter papaya leaves are sautéed with sweet shallots. Palm sugar is livened up with a dose of sour tamarind and the fire of tiny chili peppers blast holes through the pristine tranquility of coconut milk. Soon all of it will be packed up and sold door-to-door, or hawked on trains and busses, or of course sold at your friendly-neighborhood street food stall. The really excellent cooks are gossiped about and can gain quite a reputation. Before long you might see a few fat BMWs parked in front of their stalls with the well-heeled owners queueing inside.

Food vendor's peddle their trade in venues that span the gamut of shape and size. *Pikulan* are compact walking restaurants in which the cooking equipment is suspended between the ends of a bamboo pole. The pole is then hoisted onto the shoulders of the humble chef who walks along his route rhythmically beating a wooden drum or gong to announce his presence. *Kaki lima* (five legs) are three-wheeled push carts with the addition of two human legs to push them anywhere appetites are to be found.

Lesehans are sidewalk cafes that are set up entirely on the sidewalk. Starting late in the afternoon, bamboo mats are laid out, sometimes accompanied by short little tables. Roaming buskers will often serenade you as you sit on the mat and eat.

Chicken and noodles kaki lima (5-legs)

way around this is to point to what others are having, if it looks good that is. Or you can head boldly into the kitchen—they won't care—and start interrogating people. The staff will most likely have a good laugh over it.

Another interesting type of rumah makan is named after Padang, a city in Southern Sumatra where the restaurants put everything on their menus into big bowls which they then stack like a house of cards in the window. This makes it easy to spot a Padang restaurant from the outside, and inspect the food before going in. When you take a seat inside the waiter will cover your table with little bowls that replicate the variety in the window. Somehow they keep track of what you eat and present you with the bill upon finishing. Padang restaurants have sprung up all over Indonesia.

Warungs are only slightly more permanent establishments, constructed of wood and bamboo. A simple counter is enclosed by a cloth or plastic canopy that doubles as a banner to advertise the warung's specialty. Gas lamps hiss from the rafters above and illuminate a galaxy of hastily packaged consumables, bottled fizzy drinks, and the usual assortment of specialty items wrapped in banana leaves. Like lesehans, warungs often stay open until the wee hours of morning.

The next step up from the warung is the *rumah makan*, literally house of eating. When you sit down in one of these places a young boy or girl will often drop off a menu and a pad of paper and pencil. You're expected to jot down your order, but this can use up a lot of lead as they're often sold out of most what's on the menu. One

Padang style food spread in Sumatra

Nasi rames (mixed rice) in Bali

tidy and neat. Others however are downright disgusting and seem to be more interested in attracting rats than people. If you do find a warung full of people it's generally a good sign, but you should still probably heed the vendor's reluctance to feed you a particular dish you're pointing at. She might think it's a tad hot for you, or she might think it's a tad old.

Hot chili peppers make a regular appearance in many Indonesian dishes and there is never a shortage of fiery *sambal* (chili relish). Despite the reputation however, it's a mistake to assume that all Indonesian dishes are mercury busters. There are plenty of mild dishes available for sensitive palates. If you're reluctant to set your tongue on fire just say: "*saya tidak suka pedas,*" which means

There will normally be a dispenser in Padang restaurants with spoons and forks, but if you want to get the full experience of the food just use your hands as most Indonesians do. Although it's totally okay to eat with your elbows on the table, you might want to avoid excessive eating with your left hand as that's reserved for the *kamar kecil* (toilet). Bowls of water with some lime floating in them are also served. This is not a soup but rather a little *mandi* to clean your hands before and after eating.

Es dawet (also called cendol) is popular all over Indonesia

Speaking of clean, one needs to realize that eating in Indonesia is an adventure and part of the excitement is in stalking the clean warung. But don't let an initial glance deceive you as even an old and rickety warung with dirt floors and nonexistent plumbing can be quite

"I don't like it hot." If you find yourself with an uncompromising scorcher, try squeezing some lime or lemon over it to neutralize the flames. Some foods are designed to cool the heat of the chili and they are often provided at the table. One of these is *sayur acar*, a simple pickled vegetable that is often nothing more than cucumbers in sugar and vinegar, but it sure helps to cool things off.

Most street food vendors operate in shifts. For example in the mornings you can find lots of *bubur* (rice porridge) and *kue* (snack cakes and pastries). These are eclipsed by the *gorengan* (deep-fried snacks) push carts which hit the streets in the afternoons. Later on both the sweet and the meat-filled *martabak* (stuffed crepe) vendors set up and usually hang around until bedtime. Most places are happy to wrap your food *bungkus* (to go) in a variety of banana leaves, butcher's papers and plastic bags. For this it helps to grow your fingernails long as you can go quite completely insane trying to untie all those tiny knots.

If you're at home and don't feel like going out, you need only wait for the familiar call of your favorite roaming hawker. The hollow clunk of a

wooden drum might indicate the *bakso* (meat ball soup) man. A simple tapping of a spoon against a plate might signal *nasi goreng* (fried rice), and a light touch on a gong could mean the passing of a *sate* (meat kebab) specialist. Interesting little whistles and bells go on all night and some are more reliable than the local trains. They will usually have proper china, and serve your food on a tray which you can take inside the house and eat at great leisure while the vendor waits patiently outside.

With such an abundance of inexpensive and delicious food everywhere you turn, it's a wonder how anyone ever learns to cook for themselves. Why even bother with a kitchen? But the traditions of the family are strong and most Indonesians seem to have an instinctual ability to cook. Happily the legacy of preparing and enjoying bazillions of great foods continues to be passed down.

Refreshing beverages served every afternoon

Javanese nasi rames (mixed rice)

Introduction

Secrets of the Bumbu

The preparation of an Indonesian meal usually begins with the crushing of fresh spices and herbs into a spice paste known as a *bumbu*. This hand grinding is accomplished with a *cobek* and *ulek ulek* (mortar and pestle) which pulverizes the ingredients and creates a gestalt between them that is hard to match using a food processor or blender.

Not to worry however if you don't have access to a mortar as most novices won't notice the difference. You can always use a food processor, or simply mince things up into ultra-fine little bits. For a more authentic effect, run the bits over a few times with a dough roller to mash them together a little. If a blender is used it will probably be necessary to add additional liquid to get things going. Depending on the recipe add water, oil or coconut milk, and compensate by using fewer liquids later. You can also run your bumbu ingredients through an electric or hand-cranked meat grinder for results similar to a mortar.

The cobek (mortar) is indispensable when it comes to grinding bumbus

Buying a Mortar. Mortars can be found in a variety of ethnic markets as well as some kitchen shops. Indonesian cobeks come in two varieties. One is hand-chiseled from volcanic stone and the other made from a terra cotta clay. You might locate an authentic cobek in a Dutch market or a very similar one sold by an Asian grocer. One substitute is the Mexican metate. However because it's intended for grinding corn, it's often too coarse for seeds and the like. White porcelain mortars imported from China are useful here for busting up the fine stuff.

Seasoning. To season a new mortar, scrub and rinse it well with water and allow it to dry. Next drop a couple of cloves of garlic in and start crushing them with the pestle. Work the garlic into the porous surface of the mortar with circular motions. Do this for a few minutes before scrubbing out the residue and allowing to dry.

Some seeds such as cumin and coriander are best grilled first in a dry wok. This will make them crisper and easier to crush as well as more aromatic. Just heat a wok without oil and throw in a few tablespoons of seeds. Stir them constantly for just a few minutes until they darken.

The recipes in this book list bumbu ingredients in the order in which they should be ground. In general you should start by grinding the smaller seeds and nuts. Use short back and forth motions, pushing down and pivoting the pestle as you go. Next grind the tough fibrous stuff like ginger and lemon grass. Follow these with the moist elements such as garlic and shallots. Next add the liquid ingredients like tamarind water and vinegar. Dry spices like *terasi* or powdered turmeric can be added last. If the mortar is small, you may have to split the quantities up and recombine them later.

Cleaning. A good scrubbing with a brush and rinsing with hot water is sufficient to clean your mortar as most spices are antiseptic by their very nature and tend to discourage bacteria.

Grinding. It really isn't all that difficult to grind a bumbu. I've seen frail grandmothers do it without breaking a sweat. If it seems like a huge chore you're probably trying too hard. First line up all the ingredients in advance. Garlic and shallots should be peeled first and the larger or more fibrous ingredients such as ginger and lemon grass should be grated or chopped into manageable pieces.

The Wajon

The most indispensable cooking vessel in all of Asia has got be the *wajon* (wok). Nearly every food stall in Indonesia utilizes one for deep frying, boiling, stir-frying or steaming. The wajon's round-bottomed design is ingenious for concentrating most of the heat in the center, which allows for fast cooking over a very hot flame. It also requires less oil than a conventional frying pan because only the area under the direct heat needs lubrication. The curving sides also make cleaning a breeze as there are no corners to get gunked up with burned food.

Frying tofu in a wajon

When you add liquids to your wok you will notice that, as it becomes fuller, the surface area of the liquid will become greater. This makes the wok very efficient when it comes to evaporation, which makes it ideal for cooking down sauces. This extra surface area also enables less oil to accommodate more of the frying things that like to float at the surface when deep frying.

Buying a Wok. The best woks are made of steel. Most Asian markets carry reasonably-priced models that are a few grades below stainless and work great. There are also a lot of aluminum woks in use but they are not as good for all around cooking. A general-purpose wok should be around 12 to 14 inches in diameter. This size is versatile for cooking large or small quantities. Be cautious of electric models as they often have built-in elements that decentralize the heat and defeat the design of the wok. Also avoid woks with nonstick coatings as they will just end up scratching. For most stoves, you will need to buy a ring to go around your heating element and provide a platform for your wok to stand on. If you have a gas range, you may be able to place the wok directly on the rack above the gas flame, but use caution, especially when frying with hot oil, as the wok might be easy to tip over. Accessories to buy include a spatula with a curved front edge that fits the curve of your wok, a large lid, and a perforated ladle for lifting deep-fried foods out of hot oil. A bamboo steamer basket is pretty handy also.

Seasoning. A metal wok should be seasoned before use. Pour a tablespoon of cooking oil into the wok and spread it around with a paper towel so that it covers the entire surface. Heat the wok until it just begins to smoke. Remove from the heat and carefully polish the hot surface with a paper towel removing any residue. Your wok is now ready for use.

Cleaning. Avoid using detergent soaps as they can wash away the thin layer of seasoning. Use hot water only to scrub off any particles. Once the surface feels smooth, dry the wok by placing it back on the heat and allowing the water to evaporate. Turn off the heat and add a teaspoon of cooking oil. Spread it around with a paper towel to polish the surface and remove any residue. Allow the wok to cool before storing.

Sauté. A technique of cooking fairly slowly over a moderate heat. Allow the wok to heat for a minute before adding the oil. If the oil smokes then the wok is too hot. You should be able to leave the kitchen for a minute or two without burning anything.

Stir-frying. This is a famous Chinese technique of cooking very rapidly over a high heat. The wok was invented for this, but you need to do a little more than just stir. The middle is where the action is and a round-faced spatula is ideal for scooping from the bottom and tossing up the sizzling hot ingredients. If you want to cut down on fat, start with less oil and as things begin to get sticky add a little water. This will steam the food more than fry it.

Deep frying. Tipping over a wok full of hot oil would be disastrous, so before you begin make sure the wok is well supported and never fill it beyond three inches below the top. Add oil to a level that will accommodate a reasonable quantity of what you intend to fry. Heat until the oil just begins to smoke. You can test the heat by dropping a kernel of rice in; it should sizzle. Carefully add and remove ingredients with a pair of tongs or a perforated ladle. It's a good idea to wear an apron and gloves and be prepared to step back when the oil spatters.

Wok accoutrements clockwise from top left: 1) bamboo steamer, 2) spatula, 3) oil strainers, 4) wok support ring

Boiling. Woks are excellent for making soups and stocks. Some recipes call for stir-frying ingredients first and then adding liquid. Always make sure you have a solid base underneath your wok.

Steaming. Little bamboo steamer baskets are inexpensive and fit perfectly inside a wok. They usually come with two or three layers and a bamboo lid. Fill the wok with enough water to reach an inch below the bottom of the basket. Once the water starts boiling you can turn down the heat a little. Items in the bottom layers will obviously cook fastest. Be sure to add more water as necessary. When finished, rinse out your steamer and scrub it with a brush. Allow it to dry completely before storing.

Bungkus Pincuk
Banana Leaves "To Go"

The banana leaf is a multipurpose wrapper for grilling, steaming and baking. It also makes an attractive and biodegradable take-away package that will contribute a nice aroma to foods. You can buy them frozen in Asian markets but once they thaw out they are really only good for cooking with.

There's more than one way to fold a banana leaf. One of the easiest is to start with the food to be wrapped on top of a square-cut leaf.

Place a second leaf on top of the first.

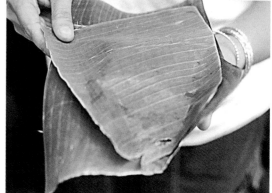

Fold the front corners over as if you were wrapping a birthday present, but instead of folding the triangle up, fold it down and under.

Repeat this with the opposite side.

Now turn the package upside down and you will find that it is actually right side up. You can secure the edges with little sticks hand-fashioned from bamboo, or you can just use a toothpick.

Introduction

INDONESIAN STREET FOOD SECRETS

PEOPLE AND PLACES

INGREDIENTS

TECHNIQUES

RECIPES

INDEX

QUIT

Clockwise from top: 1) main menu, 2) recipe menu, 3) recipe for ayam goreng (fried chicken)

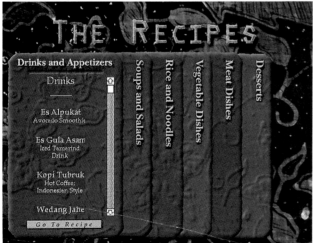

THE RECIPES

Drinks and Appetizers

Drinks

Es Alpukat
Avocado Smoothie

Es Gula Asam
Iced Tamarind Drink

Kopi Tubruk
Hot Coffee, Indonesian Style

Wedang Jahe

Soups and Salads

Rice and Noodles

Vegetable Dishes

Meat Dishes

Desserts

Go To Recipe

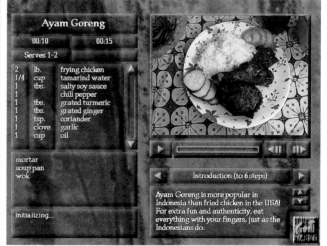

Ayam Goreng

00:10		00:15

Serves 1-2

2	lb.	frying chicken
1/4	cup	tamarind water
1	tbs.	salty soy sauce
1		chili pepper
1	tbs.	grated turmeric
1	tbs.	grated ginger
1	tsp.	coriander
1	clove	garlic
1	cup	oil

mortar
soup pan
wok

Initializing...

◄ Introduction (to 6 steps) ►

Ayam Goreng is more popular in Indonesia than fried chicken in the USA! For extra fun and authenticity, eat everything with your fingers, just as the Indonesians do.

Interactive Indonesia

www.streetfoodsecrets.com

Why bother to explore a new cuisine with all of its unfamiliar seasonings and techniques? One big return on your investment is in the fresh smells and exotic flavors that your imagination alone could never deliver. Cooking gives you a tangible, tactile experience of another cuisine, and even a subtle sense of connection with that culture.

In a similar vein the interactive nature of a CD-ROM can provide an added dimension that a book alone cannot. The movies and sounds that annotate the CD tell more of the story and provide a richer window into Indonesian cuisine. Many more ingredients and recipes than could fit into this book are included, not to mention numerous videos that document various aspects of Indonesian culture.

You will visit wonders of the ancient world, like the monuments of Borobudur and Prambanan. Watch shadow puppets play across luminous screens accompanied by gamelan orchestra. Afterwards you might take a ride in a *becak* (bicycle taxi) through an Indonesian farmer's market, or visit cottage factories and watch tofu and tempeh being made by hand. You will also encounter lots of street food chefs revealing their secrets. You can listen to them pronouncing the food and ingredient names and even learn how to order in Indonesian. In total, over 70 minutes of video documents various aspects of Indonesian food and culture, and it's all accompanied by traditional Indonesian music.

The practical advantage to having an Indonesian cookbook on your computer is that any recipe can be adjusted to fit your situation. The quantities can be customized for the number of guests you're serving, and the chili heat can be set from one to five stars. You can also print out any recipe for use as a shopping list at the market, or for in the kitchen when your fingers are covered in spice paste.

In most cases, no installation is required to play the CD-ROM. It's both Macintosh and Windows compatible. Just insert the disc into your computer's CD-ROM drive and double-click the edible-looking icon. *Selamat jalan* (happy journey)!

Street-food life in a Javanese village; each activity in this scene is linked to a video document

Central Java

Explore
Central Java

A close-up map provides links to historical monuments and cultural scenes in Central Java

Left: tour Borobudur, one of the seven wonders of the ancient world

Right: explore the ruins of Prambanan and see a performance of the Ramayana

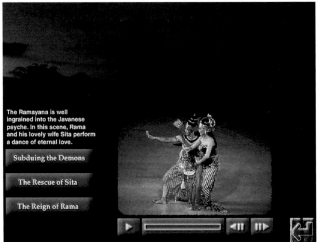

The Ramayana is well ingrained into the Javanese psyche. In this scene, Rama and his lovely wife Sita perform a dance of eternal love.

Subduing the Demons

The Rescue of Sita

The Reign of Rama

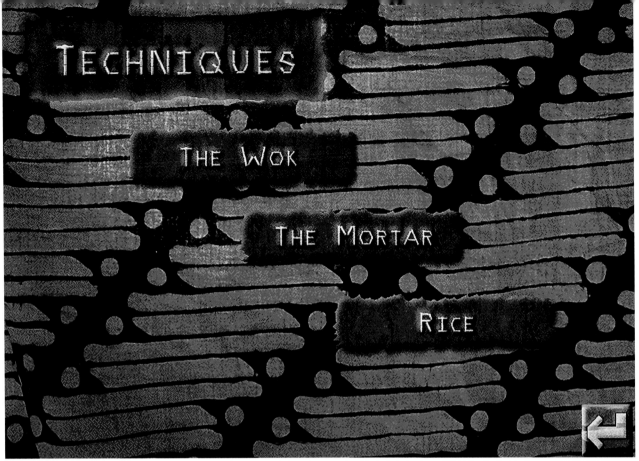

TECHNIQUES

THE WOK

THE MORTAR

RICE

The techniques section reveals secrets of the mortar and wok

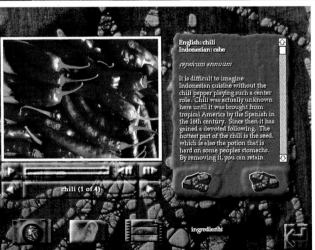

English: chili
Indonesian: cabe

capsicum annuum

It is difficult to imagine Indonesian cuisine without the chili pepper playing such a center role. Chili was actually unknown here until it was brought from tropical America by the Spanish in the 16th century. Since then it has gained a devoted following. The hottest part of the chili is the seed, which is also the potion that is hard on some peoples stomachs. By removing it, you can retain

chili (1 of 4)

ingredients

INTRODUCTION

Known as a 'wajon' in Indonesia, the wok is used throughout Asia for everything from deep-frying to making soups. The completely round bottom allows for a small amount of water or oil to facilitate the cooking of larger quantities than would be possible in a standard skillet. It also provides a variation in heat with the hot spot right in the center. This allows for the infamous technique of the super-hot stir-fry.

SEASONING

STIR FRYING

DEEP FRYING

BOILING

Ways of the Wok

Left: the ingredients section includes video and audio of Indonesian ingredients,

Right: wok techniques

Introduction

Bumbu Masakan

Ingredients

Even for the 30% of Indonesians lucky enough to own a refrigerator, it's a common practice to make a daily trip to the *pasar* (farmer's market) where only the freshest of ingredients can be selected for the next meal or two. Half the fun in going is the haggling that goes on for a price that satisfies both buyer and seller.

For the foreign visitor, the pasar offers a direct window into Indonesian community life. It's a place where you can interact with locals and practice your Indonesian immersed in an astonishing variety of goods and services.

As you walk you will encounter everything from the gargantuan knobby *nangka* (jackfruit) to the formidably spiked and notoriously redolent *durian* fruit. Fragrant cooking leaves purify air left pungent by potent *terasi* (shrimp paste). Familiar enough European vegetables bask innocently alongside gnarled rhizomes and the luminous green "body snatcher" pods of *petai*. Women in batik sarongs sort through row upon row of wooden bins overflowing with waxy candlenuts, aromatic spices, and endless piles of chilies.

In addition to stationary bins, free-lance hawkers roam the market with everything imaginable in tow. Some carry vessels of young coconut juice or balance brightly colored bottles of jamu (health potions) between the flexing ends of bamboo poles. If they don't have what you're looking for, you will eventually find it at one of the tiny food stalls peppered throughout the market. Everywhere people are offering delicious snacks to break up the shopping into manageable bites.

After experiencing this colorful pageantry, the fluorescent glow of your local supermarket will never seem as grand. However many of Indonesia's essential ingredients and spices are available with just a little effort. What can't be found in the specialty section of a large supermarket is usually available fresh or frozen at Asian grocery stores. Dried, bottled and canned versions of many ingredients can also be located and ordered on the Internet. See the links at **www.streetfoodsecrets.com** for a list of sources.

Left: the central market in Malang, East Java

ASAM
Tamarind

Tamarindus indica

Asam is the Indonesian word for "sour," and also refers to the brown seed pods that hang from shade trees found in backyards across the archipelago. A tart, gooey pulp surrounds the seeds that is used to make all kinds of things asam. *Tamarindo* is the version popular with Mexicans and you can usually find the dry pods in Hispanic markets. In Asian markets tamarind is commonly packaged as a compressed block of gummy tar.

Tamarind Water. This is the form used for most recipes so it's good to prepare a batch in advance. To make 2 cups of tamarind water, use the pulp from 5 pods, or from a 2-inch cube of the compressed gum. Combine with 1 cup of hot water. Disperse the tamarind throughout the water and mash it up with a fork. Strain the liquid and save. Repeat the process with a more water to get the remaining juice out of the leftover pulp.

BAWANG MERAH
Asian Shallot

Allium cepa L. (Aggregatum)

Shallots were probably domesticated on the mainland and brought to Indonesia by the Chinese. Indonesians also enjoy the leaves of the shallot plant lightly steamed or stir-fried. *Merah* means "red" but the taste from most any shallot is close enough for cooking. You can also substitute a red or brown onion for every 2 or 3 shallots called for.

BAWANG PUTIH
Garlic

Allium sativum

Garlic was among the earliest plants to be cultivated in Asia. It has a venerable reputation for both its gastronomic and medicinal properties. Garlic is easiest to peel if you first slice off the hard end and break the skin by crushing it with the back of a spoon. You can then briskly roll the clove between your hands to remove the peel.

CABE
Chili Pepper

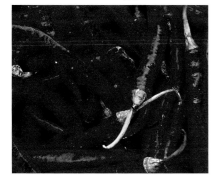

Capsicum annuum

Cabe (pronounced *chaw-bay*) plays such a dynamic and central role in Indonesian cuisine that it's hard to imagine things before the Portuguese brought it here 500 years ago. The molecule capsaican is responsible for all the excitement. It stimulates temperature-sensitive nerves on the tongue and elsewhere producing the false sensation of heat. This irritation of pain receptors is a sensation that some of us have learned to enjoy!

The heat of a particular chili can vary considerably, so until you get a feel for a particular type it is better to err on the mild side of things. The seeds are the hottest part and also the hardest on the stomach. Most Indonesians don't bother removing them, but you shouldn't feel like a woose for slicing the chili in half and scraping out the seeds. You might also substitute red or green bell peppers.

Cabe Hijau and Cabe Merah (also known as *cabe lombok).* Pile after sizzling pile of these green and red chili peppers dominate entire sections of Indonesian farmer's markets. They are long and curly as opposed to the short and squat varieties encountered in the West.

Cabe Rawit. Tiny but hot, these chilies are often directly nibbled on for contrast with fried tofu and even certain sweets. Sometimes called bird eye peppers or *nok noy* in Thai.

Cabe rawit is common in most Asian markets, but the other Indonesian varieties can be difficult to find in the West. Luckily you can replace them with common anaheim, jalapeno, or serrano varieties. Generally speaking, chilies get hotter as they get smaller, so maintaining a recipe's chili count while substituting different-sized varieties will usually result in an equal degree of hotness. One notable exception is perhaps the World's hottest chili: the habanero.

Sambal Ulek. This is red chili that has been crushed and bottled with a little salt as preservative. It keeps well and provides an easy way to add chili

to any dish. Use about 1/2 tablespoon of sambal ulek for each chili pepper called for. Also use it as a shortcut for making relishes like *sambal belado* (p. 71).

Working with Cabe. The hot oil from chilies can burn your fingers so be careful not to touch your face, eyes, and other "sensitive" body parts.

Clockwise from top left: cabe merah, hijau, kriting, and rawit

CENGKEH
Clove

Eugenia caryophyllus

These dried, immature flower buds were at one time one of the region's biggest exports. Nowadays they must be imported to meet local demand. Inhalation is the preferred method of consumption with cengkeh used only sparingly in cooking. The word kretek literally means to crackle and pop which is the sound kretek cigarettes make as they burn.

CUKA
Vinegar

Pronounced "chuka"

Vinegar was introduced from China where it has been brewed from rice for over 3000 years. Indonesian cuka is very concentrated acetic acid and is normally thinned down with water and used for making foods *asin* (sour). Any clear vinegar will work as a substitute including Japanese or Chinese rice vinegars.

DAUN JERUK PURUT
Kaffir Lime Leaf

Citrus hystrix

Leaves from the kaffir lime tree are fragrant and pleasantly sour. They should be bent and crushed a little when added to sauces in order to facilitate the release of their oils. The kaffir lime is a small, bumpy fruit that is also sometimes squeezed into foods.

Kaffir leaves are hard to find fresh, but you can sometimes find them dry. Failing that, substitute 1 teaspoon lime or lemon juice with a little of the lemon's peel for each kaffir leaf called for.

DAUN PANDAN
Screwpine Leaf

Pandanus amaryllifolius

The East's answer to vanilla, with a fresh green color and floral effect that is impossible to duplicate. Some chefs will include a few leaves when making rice for the aromatic effect. Like vanilla, pandan makes its greatest contribution to sweets

and all kinds of little green *kue* (cakes and sticky rice confections).

The leaves don't dry will, so look for them frozen and possibly labeled with their Thai name of *bai toey*. Or use the extract that has an intense green color partially due to added food coloring. One pandan leaf is equivalent to 2 or 3 drops of the extract.

DAUN SALAM
Indonesian Bay Leaf

Eugenia polyantha

Used like a Western bay leaf, but there is no substitute for the slightly sour flavor. Look for the dry leaves in Asian markets or on the Internet. Not to be confused with *Indian bay leaves* which are in fact curry leaves.

DURIAN
Durian

Durio zibethinus

A sign over the entrance to Singapore's subway reads: "No Durian Allowed." That's because the succulent flesh of this spiky fruit has a ripe and randy odor that is notorious throughout Asia. For every critic however there are scores of addicted fans who find the fruit's redolent quality inexorably linked to its charming flavor. Durian's notoriety might also be due in part to its reputation as an aphrodisiac. It is expensive on Java where population outstrips supply and the riper unsold fruit is used to flavor ice cream. Durian is hard to find fresh in the West, but it freezes well and is often sold frozen in Asian markets.

GULA MERAH
Palm Sugar

Gula merah is extracted from the sap of the *Arenga pinata* sugar palm which grows abundantly in Indonesia. There are many varieties but the distinctions hardly matter to the novice who will find any kind of palm sugar preferably to plain old white sugar. If you can't find Indonesian palm sugar you might locate a similar product from Mexico in Hispanic grocery stores. There is also a bottled brand from Thailand that resembles honey.

In most cases, brown sugar will work as a substitute. However, if the dish relies on the special charms of gula merah, you can fake it by combining equal parts brown sugar and maple syrup.

JAHE
Ginger

Zingiber officinale

Rhizomes like ginger have been utilized in Indonesia since ancient times. In addition to cooking, healers brew them into their *jamu* (health potions) with jahe being especially good for indigestion.

Measures. Recipes will usually call for the fresh grated root. Grating a rhizome makes grinding easier and simplifies the specification of quantities. One inch from an average-sized ginger root is equivalent to about one tablespoon of the grated root, which is equivalent to about 1 teaspoon of dry, powdered ginger.

Ginger and all the other rhizomes used in Indonesian cooking can be stored for long periods frozen. You can grate off as much as needed without thawing it out and return the rest to the freezer. The fresh rhizome can also be cut in thin slices and dried. In this state it can be thrown directly into soups and teas, or it can be rehydrated in hot water for 30 minutes before grinding or chopping.

JAMU
Traditional Health Tonics

One of the best approval system for a medicine is hundreds of years of trial and error. This is why researchers often turn to traditional remedies for sources of new drugs. One of the most common ingredients in jamu is fresh *kunyit* (turmeric) which accounts for its yellow and orange colors. Fresh jamus are often served in special warungs where they are mixed with a little raw egg and honey. Dry packaged jamu is available in any Indonesian drug store for everything from sexual potency to flatulence.

Ibu Riana's All Purpose Health Tonic. Slice 2 inches of fresh turmeric and an inch of fresh *kencur* into thin slivers. Boil for 15 minutes in 2 cups of water. Add some tamarind and honey and allow to cool.

KACANG PANJANG
Long Beans

Vigna sesquipedalis

Often seen overflowing from baskets and curling around the railings of Indonesian markets, kacang panjang are widely enjoyed raw for their crisp and snappy taste without the chalkiness of other green beans. They are usually harvested while the pods are still immature and eaten raw or lightly blanched in salads like *gado gado* or *lalapan*. When cooked long beans are preferred a little underdone so that the texture remains snappy. Also known as snakebeans.

Substitution. You can use any snappy green bean with relative impunity.

KAMANGGI
Lemon Basil

Ocimum basilicum (Citriodorum)

Indonesians use lemon basil for a minty contrast to *pecel* dishes, which are also usually accompanied by hot *sambal terasi*. Kamanggi is also added directly to fresh chili dips and served with soups like *soto ayam*. The leaves and flowery tops are wonderfully fragrant, and considered a good treatment for ringworm and gonorrhea! Lemon basil is easy to grow and you should be able to order the seeds on the Internet. You can find the herb in Asian markets, but it's easy to confuse with other basils used in various Asian cuisines.

If you can't find real kamanggi you can substitute Thai basil or holy basil. If all else fails combine some regular basil with fresh mint leaves.

KANGKUNG
Water Spinach

Ipomoea aquatica

Kangkung thrives in water which explains its English names of swamp cabbage, water convolvulus and water morning glory. It grows abundantly in Indonesia and is also very popular in Thailand where it is known as *phak bung*. Kangkung is rich in vitamins A and C and a good source of iron. In Indonesia it is considered a tonic for insomnia.

To cook kangkung first separate the leaves from the stems which are often tough and bitter. If the stems seem young and tender however you can chop and cook them as well.

Substitutions. Regular spinach might seem sacrilegious to an Indonesian, but it will get you by with most recipes when you can't find real kangkung.

KECAP
Soy Sauce

Pronounced "kechap"

The technique for brewing soy sauce from flour, soybeans and water was probably learned from Chinese merchants.

Kecap Asin is a close match to the standard soy sauces you'll find in any Western supermarket. The higher quality brands are brewed rather than formulated and you can test this by shaking the bottle; if a foamy head forms then it was probably brewed.

Kecap Manis is the sweet, thick sauce that lends *nasi goreng* (fried rice) it's chocolate-brown color. Next to chili sauce it's probably the most common table condiment you'll find in an Indonesian warung. Indonesian brands of kecap manis can usually be found in well-stocked Asian markets. The more common sweet soy sauces from China have an altogether different flavor. Better to cook up a batch of your own.

Making Kecap Manis. Combine 1/2 cup of brown or palm sugar for every cup of regular soy sauce. Heat this in a sauce pan until the sugar has dissolved. Add a chopped clove of garlic, 1/4 teaspoon of star anise and several thin slices of laos root. Simmer lightly for 15 minutes. The kecap will thicken as it cooks. Store in an airtight bottle.

Ingredients

KELAPA

Coconut

Cocos nucifera

Coconuts are the seeds of the coco palm and are extremely abundant on the wetter islands of Indonesia. Coconut water is used as a beverage fresh from young coconuts. *Santen* (coconut milk) on the other hand is made from the oily flesh of mature coconuts.

Kelapa Muda are the young coconuts favored for their soft, succulent flesh and sweet fragrant waters. For the ultimate virgin beverage, enterprising hawkers climb the tall, spindly trees and extract the water from coconuts still umbilicaly attached. If you can't find a young coconut, you might find cans of the beverage in Asian restaurants and markets.

Kelapa Kopyor are the créme de la créme of young coconuts. When you break open these coveted orbs you will find some of the coconut's flesh gracefully floating suspended within the liquid.

Grating coconut in a Jyogyanese market

Kelapa Tua are mature coconuts and are used to make condiments such as serundeng, or for making santen, the coconut milk used in countless recipes.

Selecting a Coconut. To insure freshness, check the "eyes" of the coconut for moldiness and make sure that you can hear liquid sloshing around inside.

Harvesting the Flesh. If you're squeamish about machetes, use a clean screwdriver or icepick to make several holes in the eyes and pour out the water (you can save it for adding to recipes in place of tap water). Place the widest section of the coconut on a flat, stable surface and smack it with a hammer or a large stone until a crack appears. Work a chisel into the opening and crack the coconut open. The white flesh can be removed by peeling it away from the shell in sections. A one pound coconut should yield about 2 to 3 cups of meat.

Dehydrated Coconut. Unsweetened desiccated coconut can be used in place of fresh coconut flesh. To rehydrate place in a bowl and cover with hot water for 10 minutes. 10 ounces of dehydrated coconut is equivalent to one fresh coconut.

Making *Santen* (Coconut Milk). Place a cup of flesh in a bowl and add an equal amount of hot, but not boiling water. Knead the flesh with your fingers for several minutes to release its oils into the water. Squeeze handfuls of the coconut

flesh over a strainer and clean bowl so that the liquid is released. If you are after a thick santen then save this as your thick batch and repeat the process with more water for a thinner batch of coconut milk. Otherwise you can just combine the two batches. 1 cup of coconut meat will yield about 1 cup of the thick and 1 cup of the thin coconut milk. An obvious modern alternative is to use an electric juicer if you have one.

Canned Coconut Milk. Generally, the cheaper the price, the thinner the santen.

Freeze Dried Santen. You can also buy powdered instant coconut milk, which is definitely convenient and not a bad compromise in terms of flavor. Simply mix the powder with warm water. Use less water for a thicker santen.

KEMIRI
Candlenut

Aleurites moluccana

Candlenuts are known as *kukui* nuts in Hawaii, where they are sometimes burned as ceremonial candles. Indonesians utilize these waxy nuts for a variety of applications from waterproofing boats to thickening sauces. You can use Macadamia nuts in place of kemiri, but where the macadamia is excellent raw, the candlenut really needs cooking to be appreciated. Kemiri is typically crushed in a mortar before cooking.

KENCUR
Lesser Galingale

Kaempferia galanga L.

This rhizome has only recently been seen outside Southeast Asia. Now you can find it frozen in some Asian markets under its Thai name of *pro hom*. Dried kencur powder is sometimes available by its Malay name of *cekur*. Failing that you can substitute the greater galingale, laos root. Medicinally kencur is used as a traditional treatment for coughs and colds and is considered a mild hallucinogen. It is also said to be good for flatulence but only when rubbed on your belly. See *jahe* for more information on working with rhizomes. Kencur makes appearances in *keredok* (p. 77), *sate lilit* (p. 101), and *opor ayam* (p. 102).

KETUMBAR
Coriander

Coriandrum sativum

Ketumbar was probably introduced from India where it has been used in curries for thousands of years. Coriander is the fruit of the cilantro plant which is easy to grow in a small pot or garden patch. For best results use whole coriander and roast it for a few minutes in a dry wok just before crushing. This will enhance the flavor and make it easier to grind it into a powder. The coriander sold in most grocery stores as a powdered spice can be used at 1/2 teaspoon for every 1 teaspoon of the whole seeds called for.

Above: the hallucinogenic properties of kencur have been wildly exaggerated

Left: after school snacks

Ingredients

KELUWEK
Pangi

Pangium edule

Keluwek bestows an enigmatic flavor and dark rich color to dishes, most notably *rawon* (p. 108). The football-shaped black nuts are native to Indonesia where they are sometimes mixed with grated coconut and used for killing rats! Somewhere along the line a clever chef discovered how the keluwak could be made deliciously edible by first boiling away its toxic properties.

If you find keluwek it will hopefully be detoxified and most likely dried. Rehydrate it in hot water before use.

KUNCI
Fingerroot

Boesenbergia pandurata

Indigenous to Indonesian, this rhizome is not easy to find in the West. You might locate it frozen or powdered by its Thai name of *krachai*, or its Vietnamese name of *ngai num kho*. If you do find the fresh root you might want to freeze some to keep it on hand. See the entry on *jahe* for more information on working with rhizomes. Kunci has a lot of healthy properties and is an ingredient in many *jamus*. It is used moderately in cooking, with a good example being *perkedel jagung* (p. 66). Where unavailable, substitute half ginger and half *laos* for kunci.

KUNYIT
Turmeric

Curcuma longa

The English were introduced to turmeric via India. The Indians probably got it from Indonesia. You can easily find turmeric in the dry, powdered form but it is far better as a fresh root. The pleasing orange color of most curries is the result of kunyit's many healthy carotenoids. These are rich in powerful antioxidants and known to improve circulation, reduce histamine levels and promote natural cortisone production. I read recently that the low incidence of Alzheimer's disease in India is thought due to a high intake of turmeric there. In Indonesia, kunyit is a prime ingredient in *jamu* health tonics.

For *jahe* for information on freezing, drying and measuring turmeric. If you stain your clothes with kunyit, hanging them out in the sun will bleach out the orange color.

LAOS
Galingale

Alpinea galanga

Also known as *lengkuas* in Java, laos is used in medicinal tonics and some even claim it has hallucinogenic properties. Because of its popularity in Thai cuisine it is becoming easier to find in Western supermarkets. The dry powder is called *galanga* in Asian markets, but it's best to use fresh laos when possible as the flavor shifts a bit as it dries. See the entry on ginger for information on measuring and freezing laos root.

LABU SIAM
Chayote

Sechium edule

Chayote is a member of the gourd family that was used a millennium ago by the Mayans of tropical America. It has a delicate, nutty flavor a bit like squash. You can substitute squash, potatoes or green papayas in recipes that call for chayote. It is also known as *jipang* in Java.

MINYAK
Oil

Deep frying is bad, okay? Well consider for a moment the contrarian view that some foods are really better off with a quick exasperating plunge into hot oil. The dramatic difference in surface temperatures seals the pores of foods against further infiltration by the oil. And according to the latest diet fad, oil is actually good for you, okay?

Sauté. Excellent, healthy oils for sautéing include olive, ghee (clarified butter), and most any vegetable oil.

Deep Frying. It's important that oil for deep frying has a high smoke point. This is the temperature at which an oil begins to burn. The higher the smoke point, the hotter the oil can get without burning. This allows foods to fry faster while absorbing less oil. Indonesians use a lot of palm and coconut oils for deep frying. Other good oils include safflower, sunflower, soybean, canola, and peanut oils. You can save oil and reuse it, but each time you do so the oil's smoke point will decrease. Oil should be replaced when it smokes before reaching 375 degrees Fahrenheit. If this seems too technical, just replace it when it starts to look scary. To prolong the life of your frying oil, turn the heat off immediately after frying. Strain out any particles before storing it in the refrigerator in a tightly sealed container. Keep in mind that any oil can become unstable and rancid long before any visible changes occur. Always keep oils refrigerated and replace them every 6 months or so.

Coconut Oil. Contrary to the bad rap it has received in recent years, research indicates that coconut oil might deserve another look. In spite of being a saturated fat, it has zero cholesterol and contains many natural antioxidants. It is also a solid at room temperature, which keeps all those fat molecules stable for long periods. Unfortunately it's difficult to find coconut oil in the West nowadays, lest it be in the form of some high-priced cosmetic intended for your hair or skin.

NANGKA
Jackfruit

Artocarpus heterophyllus

Top: hefty mature jackfruit

Right: selling young jackfruit in Java

Far right: banana vending in Sumatra

Nangka must be the largest fruit to grow in a tree. The really big ones can weigh in at over 75 pounds. They manage to reach that size by growing directly out of the trunk of the tree. Jackfruits intended for cooking are harvested when they are still immature and about the size of a large papaya. When cooked they have a nutty flavor that makes an excellent meat substitute with a texture similar to palm or artichoke hearts.

When allowed to ripen nangka tastes a little sharper than pineapple with a waxier texture and a more distinctive odor.

Canned Nangka. Your best chance of finding jackfruit in the West is inside of a can imported from Thailand. Be careful to distinguish the ripe jackfruit which is usually packed in sweet syrup. For cooking you will want the green, unripe jackfruit which is usually packed in water. Before cooking, rinse and soak the nangka in some warm salt water for 5 minutes or so to dispatch that "canned" flavor.

PALA
Nutmeg

Myristica fragrans

Nutmeg is the seed of a fleshy fruit that once grew only in the Moluccas (the spice islands of Indonesia). When ripe the fruit splits open to reveal the nutmeg seed surrounded by an aril of mace. Initially, Myristica fragrans received great fame in the West as a medicinal tonic and mild hallucinogen. Whole fresh nutmeg is vastly superior to the dry powder and can be grated directly or simply smashed in a mortar. 1 teaspoon of grated nutmeg is equal to 1/4 teaspoon of powder.

PETE
Broad Stinky Beans

Parkia speciosa

These twisted bean pods are typically several feet long and dangle from huge trees that still grow wild in the forests of Indonesia. When peeled pete vaguely resemble huge lima beans. If you hold your nose the taste is a bit like garlic with a hint of

brussels sprouts and pumpkin seeds. The raw beans are sometimes eaten directly out of the pods with or without first peeling the surrounding skin. In Indonesia pete is usually deep-fried and served with a chili sauce. It can also be stir-fried as in *pete kapri tumis* (p. 90). You will sometimes find pete frozen and by its Thai name of *sataw*. It is also sometimes spelled *petai*.

PISANG
Banana

Musa acuminata

Pisang probably originated in Indonesia where today they spring up in every available patch of earth. There are many varieties that can be divided into two main categories of those best for eating ripe, and those best for cooking with.

Pisang Ambon is the banana commonly found in Western grocery stores. It can be harvested while extremely green and keeps well during long journeys to temperate countries. Bananas have only been commonly available in such countries since the advent of refrigerated shipping. If you must cook with a banana, it is best to use one that is still quite green.

Pisang Kepok is the plantain which is often referred to by Western grocers as the "ivory banana". Plantains have a resilient texture when cooked and are best when cooked ripe. Although they remain green when ripe, you can distinguish a ripe plantain by its relative softness.

Ingredients

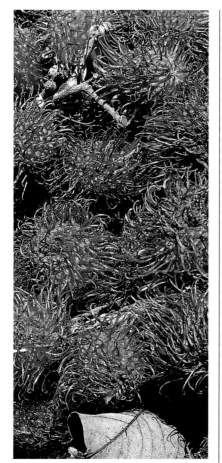

RAMBUTAN

Nephelium lappacium

Opposite: man in Lombok A translucent white fleshy fruit encased in a shell that sports a thick head of curly red hairs (*rambut* is the Indonesian word for hair). The flavor and appearance of the flesh is similar to lichee. Rambutan can be easily opened with the fingers and the flesh eaten from around its single seed. It makes a nice addition to a *rujak* (p. 78).

SEREH

Lemon Grass

Cymbopogon citratus

Popular throughout Southeast Asia, lemon grass adds a subtle flavor entirely distinct from lemons. The extracted oil is called citronella and makes a decent natural mosquito repellent. The lemon grass itself is fairly easy to grow in a pot inside the house with just a few blades pulled off as required.

Lemon grass is almost always available in Asian markets and it is starting to show up in major supermarkets as well. You can also find a dried, powdered version that is handy to keep around. Another good way to keep fresh lemon grass on hand is to freeze it and work with it directly from the freezer.

Chopping. When recipes in this book list lemon grass in inches it is meant to be cut at the base of the stalk where it is more tender and easier on the stomach. Chop it finely before grinding into bumbus.

Bruising. When a recipe calls for a bruised stalk of sereh, first peel off any dried-up blades before bruising the remaining stalk with a pestle or big spoon. Twist it around and tie it in a knot to facilitate the release of fragrant oils. You can also make an excellent tea this way. Just boil the bruised stalk of sereh in two cups of water for about 10 minutes.

Substituting. One inch of lemon grass is equivalent to about one teaspoon of the dry powder. If you can't find the powder then use about 1 tablespoon of lemon juice for each stalk called for.

SINGKONG

Cassava

Manihot esculenta

Cassava is the source of tapioca and was brought from South America. The leaves of singkong are popular in Indonesian stir fries and are amazingly high in protein. They should never be eaten raw. The root is a staple food on some of the more arid islands of Indonesia where rice cannot be grown. The plant is mildly toxic and the root should be peeled before cooking and never eaten raw. It contains the theoretical upper limit of starch by dry weight which explains why tapioca flour is so useful for gluing things together. Substitute *kangkung* or spinach for singkong leaves.

TERASI

Shrimp Paste

This fermented extract of shrimp is despised by some due to its pungent odor and fishy taste. With a little moderation however terasi can be used without detection. You might soon even find yourself craving a little more of it each day. In some foods terasi can be used like a natural MSG to add a certain definition that brings other flavors into sharp focus. Also spelled *trassi* and called *balachan* in Malaysia and *kapi* in Thailand.

Cooking. Terasi is sold in a raw form that should be cooked before consumption. For convenience prepare enough for 2 or 3 months by simply toasting it directly in a dry wok or a frying pan for about 5 minutes. Open a window and turn on a vent because the air will soon grow pungent with it. For fewer odors, wrap 2 tablespoons of raw terasi in aluminum foil and bake it in an oven at 400 degrees for about 20 minutes. Store cooked terasi in an airtight container.

Substitutions. Anchovy paste is not nearly as strong as terasi so you'll want to double the quantity.

Lauk Pauk
Friends of Rice

Other than a few closely guarded secrets, the majority of the street food chefs I encountered were extremely generous with their magic. They even suggested that I come to their homes to watch them prepare dishes bound for the streets the next day. One secret ingredient I encountered again and again was *bercanda*; the playfulness that is so well ingrained into the Indonesian psyche.

This playfulness goes hand in hand with a very relaxed attitude regarding measurements, ingredients used, and even the name of a dish. There are a few basic rules of thumb however that seem to remain fairly consistent. For example a *kari* typically designates a combination of spices very close to the Indian concept of curry. The *gulai* can be very similar but on balance uses fewer spices and is more of a soup than a sauce. An *opor* is like a thicker gulai with the addition of coconut milk, and a *sambal goreng* is like an opor with a high-octane chili presence.

A common theme throughout is the contrasting of four basic flavors: *manis* (sweet), *asin* (sour), *pedas* (hot) and *pahit* (bitter). For example salted coconut milk will be poured over sweet sticky rice, or sour fruits will be combined with a dressing that is both sweet and chili hot. Indonesian food is also full of textural contrasts. Even a simple bowl of smooth rice porridge is garnished with crunchy peanuts, flakes of fried chicken, crisp fried shallots, and crushed, crunchy *krupuk* (prawn crackers).

The ultimate feast of variety is a Dutch invention known as the *rijstaffel* for "rice table," which incorporates dozens of dishes along with all the trimmings. Every meal can't be a rijstaffel, but when designing larger meals it's worthwhile to consider contrasting these four basic flavors. The Indonesian answer to all this is *nasi rames*, which translates roughly to "rice with a little of this, and a little of that."

Quantities and Heat. Recipes printed herein are intended to serve four people. Double or halve the quantities to suit your needs. If you're worried about making food too hot for your guests, just cook with less chili but be sure to include a side dish of spicy sambal for those who like it hot. And don't forget the cooling agents that provide relief for the burning tongue and lips such as sliced cucumber, bean sprouts, *acar campur* (pickled vegetables), and fresh lime. For more precise control of quantity and spiciness you can use the CD-ROM to automatically adjust a recipe for the number of people served and the chili-dosage factor.

Clockwise from top left: 1) Dutch-style rijstaffel, (rice table), 2) lunch at Borobudur, 3) Balinese makanan

Minuman
Beverages

Drive around for a while in Java or Sumatra and you will eventually see piles of young coconuts lying along the roadside. Pull over and the seller will assist you in determining which coconut produces the coolest sound when knocked on, and which has the most promising slosh of liquid inside. He or she will then skillfully hack a flat base suitable for standing on the table, and a small opening at the top for the insertion of a spoon and straw. Between sips you can scrape at the soft flesh and eat it with the spoon.

Minuman carts offer endless permutations of the cool and refreshing variety

When making the drink for larger crowds, vendors mix the water and flesh from many young coconuts in a large basin with huge icebergs of frozen water. In addition to the young coconut's meat, they will also sometimes add other fruits like sweet jackfruit, papaya, mango, and avocado.

Despite the invasion of Western-style bottled sugar waters, cool and icy Indonesian drinks remain the number one choice among locals. Abundant rainfall and tropical heat provide the ideal climate for a bounty of tropical fruits that are utilized in icy drinks and blended into smoothies.

There is also an entire category of minuman that provides cool relief with the added dimension of slippery textures for the tongue and throat. Cubes of agar agar jelly, smooth-green rice-flour noodles, and the swollen gelatinous hulls of basil seeds are but a hint of what's to be enjoyed suspended in colorful liquids.

Some of these drinks have medicinal properties that will cool you down or heat you up. Further into this vein are the many *jamus*; the health potions which are widely consumed.

Despite the heat, hot drinks are also popular. In some areas the evenings are cool or even cold by Indonesian standards and on such a night there is nothing like a nice warm ginger tea or coffee.

ES KELAPA MUDA

Young Coconut Nectar Drink

Wherein slithers of slippery young coconut cool and satiate beyond where mere liquids can go.

2 cups water from a young coconut
1/2 cup young coconut flesh
ice

- Take the water from a fresh, young coconut.

- Scrape slithers of coconut flesh and combine with the coconut water in a glass with a little ice.

ES TELER

Mixed Fruit with Ice

Teler literally means "intoxicated" and you might find it so with the right combination of fruits.

1 cup coconut milk
1 pinch salt
1/2 cup chopped avocado
1/2 cup sweet jackfruit (ripened)
1/4 cup sweet condensed milk
shaved or crushed ice

- Make the coconut milk from a mature coconut or buy it canned. Heat to a gentle simmer being careful not to let it curdle. Dissolve in the salt and allow to cool.

- Fill each glass with ice and add the tropical fruits. Cover each with 1/4 cup coconut milk and 1 tablespoon of sweetened condensed milk.

CENDOL
Slithery Green Jelly Noodles

The secret to making these noodles is in having a sieve with holes about 1/4 inch in diameter. In Java they make a special bucket with holes drilled in the bottom, and a plunger to push all the cendol through. You can make something similar, or just use a colander with round holes. Substitute sago palm flour for tapioca flour.

1/2 cup tapioca flour
1/2 cup rice flour
2 pandan leaves
   or 5 drops pandan extract
2 cups water
1 large bowl ice water

- Mix the two types of flour before blending in 1 cup of water to make a batter.

- Bring 2 cups of water and the pandan leaves or extract to a boil in a large saucepan.

- Add the batter and reduce the heat. Simmer for 15 to 30 minutes. Stir often and keep adding water so that the mixture remains the consistency of a thin pudding. The cendol should turn dark green and become rubbery.

- Position the sieve over a bucket or large bowl filled with ice water. Pour the batter through the sieve and let the cendol drip through the holes and into the water. Squish the last of the batter through the holes and let the cendol noodles harden in the ice water for 15 minutes.

- Store refrigerated.

ES CENDOL

Coconut Milk with Slithery Green Jelly Noodles

Cendol jelly noodles have the essence and color of the pandan leaf. Make them yourself or find them ready-made in your friendly neighborhood Asian market. The Vietnamese variety called *Bahn Lot* can sometimes be found frozen.

2 cups cendol noodles (p. 56)
1/4 cup palm sugar
1/2 tsp. salt
1 cup coconut milk
2 cups ice

- To make the syrup heat 1 cup of water in a saucepan and dissolve in the palm sugar.

- In a separate pan combine the coconut milk and salt. Simmer for a few minutes.

- Allow both syrup and coconut milk to cool.

- Pour 2 tablespoons of syrup into each glass. Add 1/4 cup of cendol jelly noodles and pour the coconut milk over the top. Add ice cubes if desired.

ES SODA GEMBIRA

Happy Soda

Nice with all kinds of fizzy beverages.

1/4 cup sweet condensed milk
2 bottles soda water
ice

- Pour 2 tablespoons of condensed milk down the edges of each glass. Make a fancy pattern if you want to get artsy.

- Add ice and soda water.

ES JERUK KELAPA
Iced Citrus Drink with Coconut

Jeruk refers to any variety of citrus but es jeruk is usually either a lime or an orange that can be squeezed quickly in street stalls and mixed with a little sugar and water. For that added textural dimension include some slippery floating slivers of fresh coconut flesh.

4 medium oranges, limes, or lemons
1 cup fresh young coconut flesh
4 Tbs. sugar
ice

Opposite left to right: pineapple, sirsak, and avocado smoothies

- Combine roughly 1 part fresh-squeezed citrus juice with 4 parts water.

- Typically a few spoonfuls of sugar are added and let float to the bottom of the glass so that the sweetness can be adjusted with a little stirring.

- Add the coconut flesh and ice.

JUS BUAH-BUAHAN
Fruit Smoothies

Popular fruits and vegetables used in *jus* warungs include *pepaya*, *nanas* (pineapple), *pisang* (banana), *tomat*, *wartel* (carrot), *timon* (cucumber), and *apokat* (avocado). *Jus apokat* is usually mixed with sweetened chocolate condensed milk. This is also quite grand in a papaya or banana smoothie. You can add chocolate to condensed milk or use chocolate syrup to get similar results. Any *jus* can be ordered *campur* (mixed) with other juices. Common mixtures are carrot with apple, cucumber with tomato, or papaya with banana.

2 cups of your favorite fruit
2 cups water
1 Tbs. sugar
1 cup chopped ice
optional:
 2 Tbs. chocolate condensed milk.

- Remove disagreeable seeds and skins and blend the fruits and veggies with water, sugar and ice.

- Add a swirl of chocolate if desired.

ES GULA ASAM

Iced Tamarind

One of the secrets to cooling off on a hot day or after an especially spicy dish is to ally yourself with the engaging tartness of tamarind.

1/4 cup sugar
1 cup tamarind water (p. 38)
1 cup water

- Make a tamarind syrup by dissolving the sugar into the tamarind water in a saucepan. Simmer for several minutes. This mixture can be cooled and stored in the refrigerator for later use.

- To prepare the es asam, combine 1 part tamarind syrup with 1 part water. Serve over ice with extra sugar on the side for those who like it sweet.

BAJIGUR
Ginger Coconut Coffee

Like most recipes, this one comes in myriad combinations. Some warungs add a layer of sweet bread cubes instead of coconut.

1 inch fresh ginger, sliced thinly
1/2 tsp. grated fresh nutmeg
1 stick cinnamon
2 cloves
1 inch lemon grass, minced
4 Tbs. coffee, powdered
1 cup coconut milk
2 Tbs. palm sugar
1/2 tsp. salt
4 Tbs. young coconut flesh

- Heat the ginger, nutmeg, cinnamon, cloves and lemon grass in 3 cups water. Simmer lightly for 10 minutes.

- Turn off the heat, add the ground coffee and allow to steep for a few minutes.

- Strain the solids from this liquid and add the coconut milk, palm sugar and salt. Simmer gently for 2 minutes.

- Add the coconut flesh and a sprinkle of nutmeg on top.

KOPI TUBRUK

Indonesian Coffee

The secret to preparing excellent Indonesian coffee is to grind the beans as fine as powder. This results in their swift descent to the bottom, and you won't get that gritty taste in your mouth. Typically kopi will be mixed with enough sugar to kill a Komodo dragon. If you want it black, ask for it *pahit* (bitter). To make *kopi jahe* (ginger coffee), just throw in a few slices of ginger while you're boiling the water.

8 Tbs. coffee, powdered
4 Tbs. sugar

- Spoon in 2 tablespoons of coffee for each glass along with any desired sugar.

- Pour boiling water over the grounds and stir. Allow to stand for a minute before drinking.

BANDREK

Spiced Ginger Tea

The soothing effects of ginger make a nice nightcap. Some people like to add warm milk, either cow's or coconut, to their bandrek.

1 inch fresh ginger, sliced thinly
1 inch lemon grass, minced
2 Tbs. palm sugar

- Heat the ginger and lemon grass in 4 cups water. Simmer lightly for 10 minutes.

- Strain the boiled liquid and add the palm sugar.

Makanan Kecil

Snacks and Condiments

*Left to right:
1) girl in warung,
2) krupuk bin,
3) tofu in various guises,
4) kue lady in Java market*

How can Indonesian society support such a vast legion of street food hawkers without resulting in the obesity so prevalent in the West? Eating light and eating often might be part of the secret to staying trim. Indonesian restaurants never serve the monster quantities so typical in America. Perhaps in order to save room for the next delicacy, Indonesians seem to prefer smaller, snack-sized portions.

You might say that all Indonesian street food is *macanan kecil*, or small foods. Even servings of main dishes like fried rice or chicken sate, tend toward the petite. For small appetites the possibilities are unlimited for satisfying any tiny craving. Every warung is well stocked with mysterious little banana leaf packages and wide-mouthed jars full of odd little cakes and crackers. There is always something small and novel to snack on.

If however you are determined to spoil your supper, just add a little rice or some fried noodles and make a meal out of any of these snacks. For larger feasts all of these condiments and snacks are suitable as appetizers or side dishes in any combination. The *sambals* and other sauces listed are not usually sold separately by street food vendors, but at home you can prepare some in advance of any foreseeable snack attack.

Fried vittles Indonesian style

GORENGAN
Batter-fried Veggies

Gorengan vendors come out just as things are starting to cool down in the afternoon. They dip tofu and tempeh into a batter full of carrots and bean sprouts, and even fry up dumplings of pure batter which are pretty tasty.

Batter:
   1 cup wheat flour
   1/2 tsp. baking powder
   1 egg
   2 cloves garlic, minced
   2 shallots, chopped
   1 pinch salt and pepper
   1/2 cup parsley, chopped
   1 carrot, grated
   1/2 cup bean sprouts

1/2 lb. tofu, 1-inch cubes
1/2 lb. tempeh, 1/2-inch by 3-inch sheets
oil (for deep frying)

- Cut the tofu into 1-inch cubes and the tempeh into sheets 1/2 inch thick and 3 or 4 inches square.

- Mix the flour with 2 cups water and beat in the egg. Add the rest of the batter ingredients and enough water to create a thick batter.

- Dip pieces of tofu and tempeh into the batter. You can also make small dumplings directly out of pure batter. Fry until golden brown.

KRUPUK

Tapioca Crackers

Light, crispy krupuk consist of tapioca or sago palm flour flavored with everything from shrimp (*udang*) to fish, garlic, and soybeans. When raw, krupuk are like hard little shards of plastic. Drop them in hot oil and they instantly expand like some cheap magic trick into puffy clouds of perfectly agreeable crunchiness. Krupuk in various incarnations are usually left out in large bins at your table for eating with a meal. They are also crushed up and sprinkled over dishes like *gado gado* and *bubur* (rice porridge) as a garnishing.

Making krupuk is easy. See page 28 for tips on deep frying.

1/2 lb. dry krupuk
2 cups oil (for deep frying)
1 pinch salt

• Heat the oil in a wok for deep frying. Using a large spoon or ladle, carefully lower 3 to 10 krupuk into the oil. They will swell to many times their original size, so plan accordingly to allow room for each to float on top of the oil.

• Remove the krupuk after 20-60 seconds of frying. The krupuk will turn golden brown. Strain on paper towels.

• Sprinkle a pinch of salt on the krupuk and allow them to cool. Store in an airtight container.

REMPEYEK

Indonesian Peanut Brittle

This crunchy snack can be made with all kinds of
fillers. Besides peanuts a common favorite is
rempeyek teri which uses tiny dried anchovies.

1 tsp. coriander seeds, ground
1/2 cup rice flour
1 pinch salt
1 cup water
1 clove garlic, finely chopped
1/4 lb. roasted peanuts
2 cups oil (for deep frying)
optional:
   1 Tbs. sambal ulek

- Combine the coriander with the rice flour
  and salt in a mixing bowl. Slowly add water to
  create a runny batter. For spicy *rempeyek*, add
  sambal ulek.

- Mix the garlic and peanuts into the batter.

- Heat the oil in a wok for deep frying (see *page
  28*). Using a large spoon or ladle, carefully pour
  enough batter into the oil so it spreads out in a
  thin layer about 3 inches wide. If it balls up,
  then the oil isn't hot enough, or you may need
  to thin the batter with water.

- Turn the *rempeyek* once after about 30 seconds.
  Fry for another 20 seconds before carefully
  removing with tongs.

- Drain on a paper towel. Sprinkle salt on the
  rempeyek and allow them to cool. Store in an
  airtight container.

PERKEDEL JAGUNG

Corn and Shrimp Fritters

Bumbu:
- 1 tsp. coriander seeds, roasted
- 1 Tbs. grated kunci (fingerroot)
- 2 cloves garlic
- 1 chili pepper

1/2 cup shrimp, finely chopped
2 spring onions, finely chopped
1/2 cup corn kernels
1 Tbs. white sugar
1 pinch salt & pepper
2 cups oil (for deep frying)
1 egg
1 cup corn flour

- Grind the bumbu and combine with the remaining ingredients, beating in the egg and sifting in the corn flour last. Add water if necessary to create a thick batter.

- Fry as with perkedel kentang.

PERKEDEL KENTANG

Potato Fritters

You can use all kinds of critters to make Indonesian fritters. This potato and corned beef variety may have evolved from the Dutch kroket, or visa versa.

1/2 lb. boiled potatoes, cooled
Bumbu:
- 1/2 tsp. cumin seeds, roasted
- 2 cloves garlic
- 1 shallot
- 1/2 tsp. grated nutmeg

1/4 lb. corned beef
1 pinch salt and pepper
1 egg
2 cups oil (for deep frying)
optional:
- 1 Tbs. sambal ulek

- Grind the bumbu and mash it together with the potatoes.

- Add the rest of the ingredients, beating the egg in last. Add the *sambal ulek* only if you like your perkedel spicy.

- Heat the oil in a wok or deep fryer. Spoon out enough batter to make a fritter about 1 inch in diameter. Add as many fritters as can float to the surface of the oil. Deep fry until golden brown.

MARTABAK DAGING

Savory Mutton-Stuffed Pockets

A huge shortcut here is to buy frozen eggroll wrappers ready-made in Asian markets. The taste is similar and you won't have nearly as much fun.

Dough:
- 1 Tbs. baking powder
- 3 - 3 1/2 cups flour
- 1/2 tsp. salt

Bumbu:
- 1 onion
- 2 cloves garlic
- 1 Tbs. grated ginger
- 1 inch lemon grass
- 1 tsp. coriander seeds, roasted
- 1/2 tsp. black pepper

1 lb. ground mutton

1 cup chopped spring onions

1/2 cup chopped parsley

3 eggs

- To make the dough combine baking powder and salt with 1 cup flour and 1 cup warm water in a mixing bowl. Slowly add flour until the dough is dense enough to be lifted out of the bowl. Cover your hands and working surface with flour and knead. Keep adding flour, stretching, twisting and flattening it to establish the dough's gluten. It is ready when smooth and elastic and when it no longer sticks to your fingers. Allow to sit in a warm area for 20 minutes.

- Grind the bumbu and sauté it briefly in oil. Add the mutton and brown. Add the spring onions and stir-fry 5 minutes.

- Mix up the parsley in a bowl with the eggs before scrambling this in with the meat. Cook until eggs are done.

- Roll out a 3-inch blob of dough with a roller until it is very thin. You can do this by hand if you are qualified (see picture).

- Place rolled dough on a hot grill. Spread about 4 table-spoons of meat on half of the dough. Fold the other half over to form a pocket. Cook for about 4 minutes on each side adding oil as necessary.

Making martabak daging in Bandung, Java

Snacks and Condiments

BAWANG GORENG
Fried Shallot Flakes

Will add a decorative not to mention crunchy dimension to all sorts of noodles, salads, and rice dishes. Fry up a bunch in advance and store in an airtight container.

6 shallots, diced
   or:
2 medium onions, diced
1 Tbs. salt
2 cups oil (for deep frying)

- Dissolve the salt into 2 cups of boiling water and blanch the shallots in this for 30 seconds.

- Preheat the oil in a wok until it just starts to smoke. Fry the shallots until golden brown.

- Remove with a strainer and drain on a paper towel.

SERUNDENG
Spicy Coconut and Peanuts

Suitable for transforming an ordinary bowl of white rice into a minor feast.

Bumbu:
   1/2 tsp. cumin seeds, ground
   1 Tbs. grated laos (galingale)
   3 chili peppers
   2 cloves garlic
   1 shallot
1/2 tsp. *terasi* (shrimp paste)
1/4 lb. roasted peanuts, chopped
5 oz. grated coconut
1 Tbs. palm sugar
2 Tbs. tamarind water
1 tsp. oil

- Grind the bumbu. Chop the peanuts into quarter-sized pieces. Combine all remaining ingredients in a bowl and mix.

- Coat wok lightly with oil and heat to a medium temperature.

- Add the serundeng mixture and stir it vigilantly for 5 to 10 minutes. As the mixture heats it will dry out and the coconut will become flaky and golden brown.

SAMBAL TOMAT

Spicy Pecel Sauce

Served with *pecel lele* (p. 111) in the warung of Pak Purwanto, Yogyakarta.

8 chili peppers
1/2 cup peanuts
2 clove garlic, minced
2 shallots, minced
1 tomato, sliced
2 Tbs. oil
1 pinch *terasi* (shrimp paste)
1 pinch salt
1 Tbs. palm sugar

• Chop all the ingredients and sauté in oil for 5 minutes.

• Allow to cool before grinding everything in a mortar, blender or food processor.

BUMBU GADO GADO

Peanut Dressing

Although designed to accompany gado gado (p. 77), you might find yourself hopelessly addicted to this bumbu as a general-purpose dressing. You can substitute crunchy peanut butter for the roasted peanuts.

1 tsp. salt
1 clove garlic
1 Tbs. fried shallots
2 chili peppers
1 Tbs. palm sugar
3/4 cup roasted peanuts

• Grind the ingredients in the order listed. If using salted peanut butter, you won't need to add any salt.

• Add a little water and blend to the consistency of a gravy.

Snacks and Condiments

SAMBAL BAJAK
Coconut Chili Relish

Wherein the raging passion of the chili pepper is subdued by the velvety softness of coconut milk.

Bumbu:
   3 candlenuts
   3 cloves garlic
   3 shallots
   6 chili peppers
   1/2 tsp. shrimp paste
1 Tbs. oil
1/2 cup coconut milk
1 Tbs. palm sugar
1 tsp. salt

- Grind the candlenuts, garlic, shallots, and chili peppers together with the shrimp paste.

- Heat the oil in a wok and sauté this paste for 2 minutes.

- Lower the heat and add the coconut milk, palm sugar and salt. Cook over low heat for 10 minutes, stirring occasionally.

- Store refrigerated in an airtight container.

SAMBAL KECAP
Sweet Chili Relish

Sweet and simple...and hot! A little dab of this gooey-black madness goes miles towards enlivening an ordinary meal. Often served with *sate daging* (beef kebab, p. 100).

2 shallots
12 bird peppers
1/2 cup sweet soy sauce
1 Tbs. lime juice

- Peel and mince the shallots. Slice the bird peppers into thin rounds.

- Mix with the sweet soy sauce and lime juice.

SAMBAL TERASI

Fresh Chili Sauce

This sambal is often ground fresh with a mortar and pestle just before serving. *Terasi* (shrimp paste, p. 51) is the secret ingredient that gives this sambal a sharp twang that can grow on you.

2 clove garlic
2 shallot
8 chili peppers
1/2 tsp. *terasi* (shrimp paste)
1 squeeze lime juice

- Grind the ingredients in the order listed.

- Squeeze a bit of lime over it and serve. This sambal keeps well in an airtight container.

SAMBAL BELADO

Fried Tomato Chili Sauce

In addition to being a great stand-alone salsa, belado is the base for an entire array of chili dishes. See *terong goreng belado (p. 93)*, and *ayam belado* (p. 104).

4 cloves garlic, chopped finely
4 shallots, chopped coarsely
2 Tbs. oil
1 inch laos root, sliced thin
2 tomatoes, diced
30 chili peppers, chopped
 or 2 cups *sambal ulek (p. 39)*
1/2 cup sweet soy sauce
1/4 cup palm sugar
2 salam leaves
1 tsp. salt

- Heat the oil in a wok and sauté the garlic and shallots for 2 minutes.

- Add remaining ingredients to the wok and simmer for 5 minutes.

- Remove from the heat and allow to cool. Store in a tightly sealed jar and refrigerate.

Sop, Soto, dan Sayur Segar
Soups and Salads

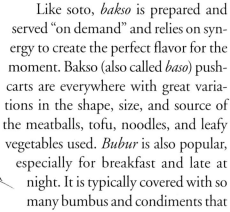

Indonesian soups can be divided into two categories: *sops* and *sotos*. A sop is similar to a Western soup with a clear broth and some ordinary looking vegetables. Sotos venture into much less familiar waters to include chilies, sour galingale, lemon grass, and sometimes coconut milk. While a sop might provide comfort on a cold winter's day, sotos are more the ticket for a hot one. Between the actual temperature of the soto and the chilies it contains, you might break into a sweat powerful enough to make even a puny breeze feel downright cool. Sotos are also open to improvisation by the server. Where a sop will be ladled straight away from a single stock pot, sotos tend to be assembled from their components on the spot.

First cooked noodles are added to an empty bowl and covered with a broth from one pot and some meat from another. Various vegetables are added and allowed to steam in the bowl while splashes from different bumbus cover them. Finally an assortment of garnishes tops things off.

Like soto, *bakso* is prepared and served "on demand" and relies on synergy to create the perfect flavor for the moment. Bakso (also called *baso*) pushcarts are everywhere with great variations in the shape, size, and source of the meatballs, tofu, noodles, and leafy vegetables used. *Bubur* is also popular, especially for breakfast and late at night. It is typically covered with so many bumbus and condiments that it's easy to forget it's just rice porridge.

Perhaps the most well known Indonesian salad is *gado gado*, but many other varieties abound with bumbu dressings that explore the realm between sweet, sour and hot. The bumbu is usually ground before your eyes but at home you might want to prepare enough to last a few weeks.

The combination of palm sugar, tamarind and chili peppers is one of the secrets to dealing with a sweltering day. Perhaps that's why vendors for *asinan* and *rujak* hit the streets during the hottest period and exploit this tongue-warping effect. You will no-doubt sweat off any excess calories the snack provides.

The Bakso Man

People speak softly in the cool Javanese evenings. After the purring of an occasional motorcycle, or the intermittent clucking of a cicak lizard, the loudest noise you're likely to hear is the gentle "tok...tok...tok" of the bakso man's wooden drum as he pushes his cart through the night.

SOP BASO
Meat Balls in Clear Broth

Street servings of bakso combine several sizes and varieties of meatballs. For simplicity you can find the meatballs ready-made in Asian markets.

Meatball Ingredients:
  1/2 lb. fish, beef, or pork, finely ground
  2 cloves garlic, crushed
  1 egg
  2 Tbs. tapioca flour
  1 pinch salt and pepper
If ready-made meatballs:
  2 cups meat broth.
The rest:
  1 clove garlic, crushed

1 pinch salt and pepper
2 shallots, finely chopped
2 chili peppers, chopped
1 Tbs. palm sugar
1 cup cooked egg noodles
1 cup kangkung or spinach
1 cup bean sprouts
1 Tbs. fried shallot flakes

- To prepare meatballs; grind the garlic and mix with the meat and egg. Sift in tapioca flour, and add salt and pepper.

- Boil 4 cups of water. Grab a handful of the meat mixture and make a fist, squishing it through your thumb and index finger. Scoop out a spoonful and place in boiling water.

- If using ready-made meatballs, add them with the meat broth to 4 cups boiling water.

- Add the remaining ingredients except for the kangkung and fried shallots. Boil for 15 minutes.

- Add the kangkung or spinach during the last 3 minutes.

- Garnish with bean sprouts and fried onion flakes.

Soups and Salads

BUBUR AYAM
Chicken Porridge

Early each morning, Jakarta street venders hawk this popular dish to pedestrian commuters. Myriad chopped-up goodies are kept in separate containers and a custom bubur is prepared on the spot.

1 cup white rice
2 cups soto ayam stock (p. 75),
  or canned chicken broth
Garnishes:
  1/4 lb. chicken, shredded
  1 Tbs. spring onions, chopped
  2 Tbs. fried peanuts
  2 Tbs. fried shallots (p. 69)
  2 Tbs. Chinese donut, sliced
  2 krupuk, crushed

- Rinse rice and combine with 5 cups water. Bring to a boil, reduce heat and cover. Cook about 1 hour. When ready the bubur should be thick, but still easy to stir. If it's too dense, keep adding water.

- Meanwhile prepare the soto broth.

- Add 1 cup of rice porridge to a bowl and cover with 1/4 cup of soto broth. Garnish with anything and everything.

SOP BUNTUT
Oxtail Soup

Served in roadside *rumah makan* diners across the archipelago.

1 lb. oxtail, 1-inch cubes
2 cloves garlic, finely chopped
1 medium onion, coarsely
  chopped
1/2 cup cubed potatoes
1/2 cup sliced carrots
3 stalks celery, chopped finely
1/2 tsp. cloves
1/2 tsp. nutmeg
1 pinch salt and pepper
Garnish with:
  3 Tbs. fried onion flakes

- Use a stock pot to bring the oxtail, garlic, and onion to gentle boil in 5 cups of water. Cook for 1 hour.

- Add the remaining ingredients and simmer until the potatoes are soft.

SOTO DAGING

Hearty Beef Soup

Bumbu:
- **1 Tbs. grated turmeric**
- **2 chili peppers**
- **2 cloves garlic**
- **2 shallots**
- **1/2 cup shrimp, peeled**

1 Tbs. oil
1/2 lb. beef chuck, cubed
1 Tbs. palm sugar
1 pinch salt
3 inch ginger, sliced thin
1 tsp. lime juice
1 hard-boiled egg

- Grind the bumbu and sauté in the oil for 2 minutes before adding the beef and stir-frying for 5 minutes.

- Add 4 cups water, the sugar, salt, and ginger. Simmer 15 minutes.

- Garnish with lime and egg.

SOTO AYAM

Indonesian Chicken Soup

Bumbu:
- **1 inch lemon grass**
- **1 Tbs. grated ginger**
- **1 Tbs. grated turmeric**
- **2 cloves garlic**

2 cups chicken broth
1/4 lb. chicken, shredded
1 stalk lemon grass, bruised
1 kaffir lime leaf
2 chili peppers, chopped
1 pinch salt and pepper
8 oz. *soun* (cellophane noodles)
1/2 lemon or lime
1 hard-boiled egg, sliced
1 spring onion, chopped
1/2 cup bean sprouts
2 Tbs. fried onion flakes

- Chop an inch off the base of the lemon grass and grind with the other bumbu ingredients.

- Combine this bumbu with 2 cups of water and 2 cups chicken broth. Bring to a boil.

- Add the chicken, lemon grass, lime leaves, chilies, salt and pepper. Cook for 20 minutes.

- Meanwhile soften the soun by soaking it in boiling water.

- Add a handful of noodles to each serving bowl and cover with soto broth. Squeeze in some lemon and garnish with the remainder of the ingredients as well as anything else you can think of.

ACAR CAMPUR
Sour Veggie Relish

Crisp, cool and tangy, acar campur is perfect for extinguishing the fire. Provided of course that you avoid eating the bird peppers.

1 carrot, julienned
3 bird chili peppers
2 spring onions, 1 inch lengths
1 cucumber, julienned
1 tsp. salt in 2 cups water
2 cups vinegar
1/4 cup sugar
1 tsp. salt
2 shallots, thinly sliced
4 cloves garlic, cleaned

- Soak the carrots, chilies, spring onion and cucumber for 15 minutes in salt water. Rinse.

- Heat the vinegar in a saucepan and dissolve in the sugar and salt. Simmer the shallots, and garlic in this for 10 minutes.

- Remove from heat and add soaked veggies. Mix thoroughly.

- Allow the campur to pickle overnight or longer. Chill before serving.

LALAPAN
Raw Vegetable Platter

There's nothing so unusual about lalapan until you dip the raw veggies into hot *sambal terasi* (p. 71). If the sambal is too hot try mellowing it with a tablespoon or two of sweet soy sauce. *Kacang panjang* (long beans) are snappy in this, or any other raw vegetable that you like.

1/4 cup kamanggi
1 tomato
1 cucumber
Any raw vegetables
1/2 cup *sambal terasi* (p. 71)

- Break or chop all the veggies into bite-size pieces.

- Slice and arrange the veggies around the dip and serve. *Krupuk* (shrimp crackers) make a good complement.

KEREDOK

Salad With Peanut Sauce

The addition of *kencur* (p. 45) to this salad's dressing lends an interesting twang. Substitute galingale if you can't find kencur.

Bumbu:
  1 Tbs. grated kencur
  1 cup bumbu gado gado (p. 69)
1 cup thin-sliced cucumbers
1 cup fresh bean sprouts
2 tomatoes, sliced
2 cups lettuce

- Grind a bumbu just like the gado gado dressing, but start by adding the kencur Add a little water if necessary to thin.

- Toss the sauce with the vegetables until well mixed. Serve with a krupuk.

GADO GADO

Steamed Veggies with Peanut Sauce

The most common veggies are listed here, but you can improvise with any others. The real secret is in the peanut bumbu (p. 69).

1/4 lb. fried tofu (p. 94)
2 medium potatoes, boiled
1/4 lb. long beans
1/4 lb. bean sprouts
1 cucumber
1/4 lb. cabbage
1/2 cup bumbu gado gado
white rice or *lontong* (p. 82)
1/4 lemon
2 Tbs. fried onion flakes
2 *krupuk* (prawn crackers, p. 64)
2 hard-boiled eggs, sliced

- Fry tofu and boil the potato.

- Slice the potato and veggies into bite-sized pieces. Blanch the veggies in boiling water for 30 seconds.

- Toss all of the veggies with the peanut bumbu.

- Pile the gado gado on a base of white rice or *lontong*. Add a squeeze of fresh lemon, some fried onion flakes, sliced egg, and a crunched-up *krupuk*.

RUJAK
Sweet, Sour, and Hot Fruit Salad

Innocent sweet and tart fruits corrupted by a wicked bumbu.

Bumbu:
- **6 chili peppers**
- **1/4 tsp. *terasi* (shrimp paste)**
- **1 pinch salt**
- **2 Tbs. palm sugar**

4 Tbs. tamarind water
1/2 cup sliced hicama
1/2 cup sliced pineapple
1/2 cup sliced rambutan
Other assorted tart or sweet fruits
1 Tbs. lime juice

- Grind the bumbu and combine with tamarind water.

- Combine fruit with bumbu dressing and toss.

- Move to individual serving bowls, squeezing some fresh lime over the top before serving.

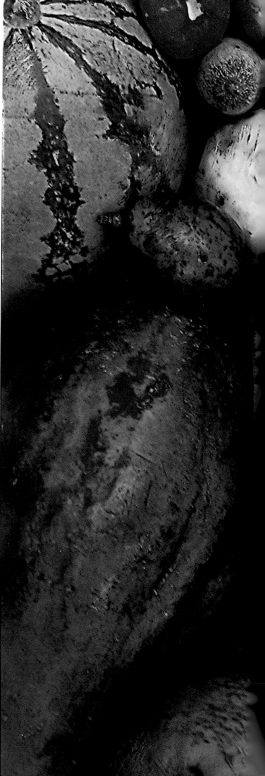

ASINAN

Fresh Salad with a Tangy Dressing

A famous Jakarta dish that is more *asin* (sour) than rujak, and uses vegetables as opposed to fruits. Try adding any salad veggies you like.

1/4 lb. egg noodles

1/2 lb. tofu, cubed

Bumbu:

   2 Tbs. *ebi* (dried shrimp)

   1/4 cup roasted peanuts

   2 chili peppers

   2 Tbs. palm sugar

   1 tsp. salt

1/2 cup vinegar

1 cup long beans

1 cup thinly sliced cabbage

1 cup bean sprouts

1 cucumber, sliced

8 cherry tomatoes, sliced

4 prawn crackers (krupuk)

- Boil the egg noodles with a little salt until soft (about 8 minutes). Drain and rinse.

- Grind the bumbu and mix with the vinegar.

- Toss the noodles with the vegetables and tofu. Toss in a few extra peanuts whole. Serve in individual bowls with krupuk crushed up on top.

Nasi & Mie

Rice and Noodles

Rice is the centerpiece of Indonesia's agricultural economy and is rarely absent from a meal. Indonesian words for rice describe its state.

Padi are the live rice plants and traditionally Indonesians believe that the padi harbors a nature spirit. A Balinese legend memorializes a sacred virgin who committed suicide rather than to give her virginity to a suitor. Her spirit remains close above the padi where her body lies buried. Villagers are respectful of this spirit and chant soothing apologies to her as the reaper harvests the padi with a small and discrete blade, so as not to frighten her.

Growing rice in the desa, East Java

Beras is dried rice, ready for cooking. You can find many variations in the texture, length of grain, color, and price of beras. Although natural brown rice is available, hulled white rice is vastly more popular. This seems partially due to the "clean" taste of white rice that goes with any meal. Also, without refrigeration the oil present in the brown rice bran can become rancid and spoil. White rice also cooks much faster that brown which is a consideration where fuel is costly. Today Indonesia is unable to meet its own demand for rice and imports millions of tons every year, much of it from Thailand. Jasmine rice from Thailand is also imported by most Western countries and is very similar to Indonesian beras. You can use any long-grain white rice.

Ketan is sticky rice and it comes in white and black varieties. It can be soaked in water overnight to soften it up, or cooked directly if time is not an issue.

Nasi is the word for cooked rice and many Indonesian dishes begin with this word to indicate its central role. A Javanese grandmother recently wrote to the Jakarta post decrying the consumption of fast food in that city. She went on to insist that a real Indonesian woman could never feel satiated on just bread and burger; she must have rice. Nasi also gives you something to squish around in your fingers and absorb all that rich and delicious sauce.

The most common way to prepare nasi is to boil the rice with water, or sometimes with coconut milk and a spice bumbu.

Rice Cookers. This is one of the few modern appliances that has quickly become a necessity with most Asians who can afford one. Because the boiling point of water is a constant, a built-in thermostat can sense the rise in temperature when all the water has been absorbed by the rice. The rice cooker will automatically switch to warming mode at this point and keep the rice fluffy and ready to eat for hours. If you're trying to make a soupy rice porridge and the cooker goes into warming mode, then you know you need to add water and set it back to cooking mode again.

Rinsing. Jasmine rice should be washed to rinse off excess starch. Cover with water and stir the rice around with your hand before carefully pouring the water out between your fingers. Do this several times until the water runs clear.

Measuring and Cooking. White rice needs about 1-1/2 parts water to 1 part rice. A secret to measuring the water is to fill the pot until the water level reaches the first joint of your index finger as it touches the rice.

Cooking. If using a rice cooker, simply turn it on and forget about it. In a stove-top pot, wait for the water to boil before covering and lowering the heat to a simmer. Cook until the water is absorbed and dimples form in the surface of the rice (about 20 minutes). Allow the rice to sit for 10 minutes before serving.

Steamed Rice. For a fragrant and plump quality, cook the rice as before, but stop when the kernels are soft (about 10 minutes). Transfer the rice to a steamer, lining the bottom with a banana leaf or clean towel if necessary to keep the grains from falling through. Steam for 20 minutes.

Microwave. This actually makes a fairly decent rice cooker. Just combine the water and white rice in a microwave bowl and cook on the highest setting for 5 minutes. Finish at the medium setting for 15 minutes.

NASI UDUK

Coconut Milk Rice

A favorite breakfast in Sumatra, where it is served with shredded omelet and fried shallots. In Java they serve it with peanuts, tempeh and krupuk.

1 cup white rice, rinsed
1 cup coconut milk
1/2 cup water
1/2 tsp. salt
1 blade lemon grass, bruised
1 pandan leaf

* Combine all ingredients and cook as with plain whit rice.

NASI GORENG
Fried Rice

Leftover rice works best because it's a little dry and crusty. If you make it fresh just use a little less water than normal.

4 cups cooked rice
2 Tbs. oil
2 cloves garlic, chopped
2 shallot, chopped
1/2 lb. boneless chicken
1 red chili pepper
2 eggs
2 Tbs. sweet soy sauce
1 cucumber
prawn crackers (*krupuk p. 64*)

- Heat the oil and sauté the garlic and shallots for 2 minutes.

- Toss in the chicken and stir-fry until hot and fully cooked.

- Add the chili peppers and scramble in the eggs.

- Next the rice and sweet soy sauce. Stir vigilantly until the kernels of rice have separated. Add a little water if necessary to keep things moving.

- Garnish with slices of cucumber and some *krupuk*.

KETUPAT DAN LONTONG
Fused Rice Rolls

Ketupat and lontong are commonly used a base for *gado gado* and *sate ayam*. They both use the same recipe but ketupat is cooked inside hand-woven coconut leaves and lontong uses a simple rolled up banana leaf. For our purposes, a plastic bag can be utilized, but you must puncture it with tiny holes to let the water in.

2 cups white rice
1 tsp. salt
4 banana leaves
  or 5-inch plastic sandwich bags

NASI KUNING
Yellow Rice

This rice is often cooked in a cone-shaped bamboo basket called a *kukusan* so that when inverted it becomes a bright volcano of *kuning* (yellow).

Bumbu:
   1 tsp. cumin seeds
   2 tsp. coriander seeds
   2 Tbs. grated turmeric
4 cups rice
1 cup chicken broth
1 cup coconut milk
4 cups water
1 cinnamon stick
2 cloves
1 lemon grass stalk
1 salam leaf

- Roast the cumin and coriander seeds before grinding with the turmeric.

- Rinse the rice and combine in a rice cooker or large pot with the rest of the ingredients. Cover and simmer. If you don't have a steamer continue cooking until all liquid is absorbed (about 20 minutes)

- If you have a steamer transfer the rice after about 15 minutes and steam it until the rice is fluffy and fully cooked (about 15 minutes).

- Banana leaf method: cut in 8 by 4-inch sections. Place 1/2 cup of rice in the center and roll it up lengthwise, creating a 4-inch cylinder with a diameter of about 1 inch. Fold the ends up and secure with a toothpick.

- Plastic bag method: fill with 1/2 cup rice and roll the bag up as tightly as possible. Secure with several rubber bands. Next use a toothpick or ice pick to make tiny holes in the surface of the bag to allow water in.

- Place the rice pockets in a stockpot and cover with water. Add the salt and cook covered at a gentle boil for 2 hours.

- Remove the lontong and allow it to cool before unwrapping.

NOODLES

Noodles have been used in Indonesia since long before they were popular in Italy. The Chinese invented them, perhaps as a way of storing rice for the long journey to Indonesia. The noodles used in Indonesian cooking are of three main varieties:

Mihun (also called *bihun*) is probably the original noodle made from rice. It goes by many names in as many lan-

guages. A very thin vermicelli is also made from rice and is sometimes used in place of *soun* (see right).

Bakmie (or just *mie*) are made from wheat flour sometimes with the addition of eggs (*mie telur*). You will find mie labeled as egg noodles, yellow noodles,

or perhaps by the Thai name of *bah mee*.

Soun is a semitransparent vermicelli made from mung bean flour. Soun adds a slithery texture to soups like soto ayam (p. 75). You will find soun labeled as glass, cellophane, or bean thread vermicelli.

BAKMI GORENG

Fried Rice Noodles

As with fried rice, these noodles are great prepared with any leftovers.

8 oz. rice noodles
2 cloves garlic, finely chopped
2 shallots, finely chopped
1 Tbs. oil
1/4 lb. boneless chicken, cubed
1/4 lb. cabbage, thinly sliced
1 Tbs. salty soy sauce
1 pinch pepper
1/4 lb. mushrooms, quartered
2 Tbs. sweet soy sauce
1 Tbs. fried onion flakes (p. 68)
2 prawn crackers (*krupuk p. 64*)

- Boil noodles until soft (about 3 minutes). Rinse and drain.

- Heat the oil in a wok and sauté the garlic and shallots for several minutes. Add chicken, cabbage, salty soy sauce and pepper. Stir-fry 5 minutes.

- Add the mushrooms, noodles, sweet soy sauce, and 1/4 cup of water. Stir-fry until mushrooms are soft and noodles are hot.

- Garnish with fried onions and a krupuk or two.

MIE GORENG

Fried Egg Noodles

The other fried noodle.

8 oz. egg noodles
2 cloves garlic, finely chopped
2 shallots, finely chopped
1/2 cup celery, chopped
1 Tbs. oil
2 chili peppers, chopped
1/4 lb. fresh shrimp
1 Tbs. sweet soy sauce
a pinch of salt and pepper

- Boil the noodles until they separate and become soft (about 8 minutes). Rinse.

- Sauté the garlic, shallots and celery in the oil for 2 minutes.

- Add the shrimp and stir-fry for 30 seconds before adding the chilies, noodles, sweet soy sauce, salt, pepper and 1/4 cup of water. Stir-fry until the noodles are hot.

KETOPRAK

Tofu and Rice Noodles in Yummy Peanut Sauce

This popular dish is often eaten for breakfast by office workers who find it in the narrow alleys between towers in Downtown Jakarta.

8 oz. tofu, deep fried (p. 94)
8 oz. rice noodles
1 Tbs. oil
2 cloves garlic, finely chopped
1/4 cup peanut butter
1 Tbs. palm sugar
1 Tbs. sweet soy sauce
1 tsp. salt
1 cup bean sprouts, cleaned

- Either bake or deep fry the tofu. Freezing it before baking will make the texture chewier.

- Boil the noodles until soft (about 5 minutes). Rinse.

- Heat the oil in a wok and sauté the garlic for a several minutes.

- Add the peanut butter, 1/2 cup water, palm sugar, sweet soy sauce and salt. Simmer for 5 minutes.

- In a fresh bowl, combine the noodles, fried tofu, bean sprouts and peanut bumbu sauce. Toss well.

- Garnish with a little sweet soy sauce and fresh bean sprouts.

LAKSA

Glass Noodles in Coconut Sauce

Indonesian Street Food Spaghetti.

8 oz. bean-thread noodles

Bumbu:
  1 tsp. coriander seeds
  1 Tbs. grated ginger
  1 Tbs. grated turmeric
  2 cloves garlic
  2 shallots
1 Tbs. oil
1/4 lb. boneless chicken, cubed

1 blade lemon grass, bruised
2 chili peppers, chopped
1/2 cup chicken broth
1/2 cup coconut milk
1 Tbs. sweet soy sauce

- Cover noodles with boiling water. Rinse after 5 minutes.

- Crush the bumbu and sauté for several minutes in the oil.

- Add the chicken, bruised lemon grass, and chopped chilies. Stir-fry for 5 minutes.

- Add the chicken broth, coconut milk, and sweet soy sauce. Simmer for 5 minutes.

- Place a serving of noodles in each bowl and cover with sauce.

Rice and Noodles

A vegetarian's paradise

Sayur Sayuran
Vegetables

It is easy to be a vegetarian in Indonesia. Plentiful rainfall and rich volcanic soil provide most of the region with a bounty of nutritious vegetables. Because most dishes gain their unique flavors from vegetable sources, just about any recipe can be made meat free. And the widespread use of soybeans for making tempeh and tofu can satisfy all necessary protein requirements.

Although a huge percentage of Indonesians live at or below the poverty level, their simple diet is far healthier than that of many Westerners. The vast assortment of sources from which they gain their sustenance also insures that all trace nutrients and minerals are consumed.

In addition to familiar vegetables, many less obvious parts of a plant are utilized. For example the leaves of the cassava, long bean, papaya and shallot are all cooked in various dishes. Many of these plant parts are used for medicinal purposes such as lowering blood pressure or bringing down a fever.

See the ingredient section for more information on sources and alternate names for the more hard to find Indonesian vegetables. If you can only find them canned, it helps to soak these vegetables in a light solution of salt water for 10 minutes before rinsing with fresh water. If all else fails many tropical vegetables can be grown indoors like houseplants for a steady year-round supply.

SAMBAL GORENG JIPANG

Chapote Stew

An ambrosial medley of flavors from the old world and the new.

1 lb. chapote, peeled
1 Tbs. salt
Bumbu:
   1 Tbs. grated turmeric
   2 cloves garlic
   2 shallot
   2 red chili peppers
   1 pinch *terasi* (shrimp paste)
1 Tbs. oil
1 small tomato, sliced
1/2 cup coconut milk
1 pinch salt

- Peel the chapote and cut it into 2-inch by 1-inch pieces. Put these in a bowl with a tablespoon of salt. Shake them around to cover them with salt and let sit for 10 minutes. Afterwards rinse and drain.

- Grind the spice bumbu and sauté in the oil for 2 minutes.

- Add the chapote and tomato. Sauté for 5 additional minutes.

- Add the coconut milk and lower the heat. Simmer for 10 minutes being careful not to curdle the milk. Add salt to taste.

- Serve with white rice.

BUNCIS KUNING

Green Beans and Potatoes in Coconut Milk

1 lb. potatoes, cubed
Bumbu:
   1 Tbs. grated turmeric
   1 Tbs. grated ginger
   1 clove garlic
   1 shallot
   1 pinch *terasi* (shrimp paste)
1 Tbs. oil
1/2 lb. green beans, 2 inch pieces
1/2 cup coconut milk
1 pinch salt

- Boil the potatoes 15 minutes.

- Crush the bumbu and sauté it for several minutes in the oil.

- Add potatoes and beans to the wok and stir-fry for 5 minutes.

- Add the coconut milk and lower the heat. Simmer for 5 minutes. Add salt to taste.

PETE KAPRI TUMIS

Stir-fry Petai Beans with Snowpeas

Petai beans (p. 49) have a unique taste that goes well with garlic and snowpeas. If they are too strong for you just substitute any other vegetable.

2 cloves garlic, diced
2 shallots, diced
1/2 Tbs. oil (for sauté)
1 cup pete beans
1/2 tomato, sliced
2 cups snow peas, trimmed
2 red chili peppers, julianned
1/2 Tbs. sugar
1/2 Tbs. sesame oil

- Sauté the garlic and shallots in the oil for about 2 minutes.

- Add the pete beans and tomato. Sauté this for a few minutes longer.

- Add the snow peas and remaining ingredients. Stir-fry until the pete is soft (about 5 minutes).

TUMIS KANGKUNG

Stir-fried Water Spinach

The recipe is basically unchanged when using kangkung or spinach.

1 lb. *kangkung* (water spinach)
2 cloves garlic, minced
2 shallots, chopped
1 Tbs. oil
2 red chili peppers, julianned
1/2 tomato, sliced
1/2 Tbs. sugar
1/2 Tbs. sesame oil

- Wash the water spinach and pluck the leaves from the stalk. If the stalk is reasonably clean and tender, you can cut it into 2-inch sections and use.

- Sauté the garlic and shallots in the oil for about 2 minutes.

- Add the water spinach and remaining ingredients. Stir-fry until the kangkung is soft (about 3 minutes).

GUDEG

Sweet Jackfruit Stew

Served in Yogyakarta, Central Java, where the cuisine is known for its sweetness. Every evening gudeg vendors lay out rattan mats on the sidewalks and until nearly daylight they will serve you gudeg with your choice of stewed tempeh, tofu, boiled eggs, chicken or beef skin. These additions are sometimes stewed in with the rest and sometimes cooked separately.

Bumbu:
    1 tsp. coriander seeds, roasted
    1 tsp. cumin seeds, roasted
    4 candlenuts
    1 Tbs. grated laos (galingale)
    2 clove garlic
    1 pinch *terasi* (shrimp paste)
1/2 lb. young green jackfruit
1 salam leaf
1 kaffir lime leaf
1 cup coconut milk
2 Tbs. palm sugar
1 pinch salt and pepper

- Grind the spice bumbu. Feel free to add chilies.

- In a stockpot, combine the bumbu with 1 cup water, the green jackfruit, and the cooking leaves. You can also add other ingredients now as mentioned above. Simmer for 20 minutes.

- Lower the heat and add the coconut milk, palm sugar, salt and pepper. Simmer 30 minutes.

LAWAR

Mixed Jackfruit Salad

A fun dish to make; you get to squish everything together with your hands.

1 lb. young jackfruit, sliced
1 cup grated coconut meat
Bumbu:
  2 candlenuts
  1 clove garlic
  1/2 Tbs. grated kencur (p. 45)
  2 shallots
  2 chili peppers
  1 pinch *terasi*, (shrimp paste)
1 Tbs. oil (for sauté)
1 cup long beans, chopped

- Grind the bumbu and sauté in the oil for 3 minutes.

- Boil the long beans and jackfruit for 3 minutes.

- Combine all ingredients and mix using your fingers.

SAYUR PEPEYA MUDAH

Young Papaya Stew

A specialty in the *warung kecil* of Ibu Dasak Nyoman at the central market in Ubud, Bali. The papaya ends up tasting like a tender, delicious squash.

1 lb. green papaya, 2-inch slices
Bumbu:
  1 tsp. whole pepper corns
  1 inch lemon grass
  2 kemiri nuts
  1 Tbs. grated kunyit
  2 cloves garlic
  2 shallot
  1 pinch terasi
1 Tbs. oil
1 salam leaf
1 small tomato, sliced
1 cup coconut milk
1 pinch salt

- Peel and cut the papaya. Shake the papaya pieces in a bowl with 1 Tbs. of salt. Set the bowl aside for 10 minutes. Rinse with water.

- Grind the bumbu and sauté in the oil for 2 minutes.

- Add papaya, salam, tomato and salt. Sauté for 5 minutes.

- Add the coconut milk and cover. Simmer for about 20 minutes. When done the papaya should be quite tender.

OSENG OSENG

Stir-Fried Vegetables

The Javanese word for stir-fry is *oseng*, which when said twice seems to convey the sense of urgency required.

2 cloves garlic
2 shallots
1 pinch *terasi* (shrimp paste)
1 Tbs. oil (for sauté)
1 small tomato, sliced
1 cup baby corn, sliced
1 cup bok choy, chopped
6 red chili pepper, julianned
1/2 Tbs. sugar
1/2 Tbs. sesame oil

- Heat the oil in a wok and sauté the garlic, shallots and terasi.

- Add the tomato and baby corn. Stir-fry for 3 minutes.

- Add the remaining ingredients and *oseng oseng* for 5 minutes.

TERONG GORENG BELADO

Fried Eggplant in Spicy Tomato Sauce

These are the long skinny "Japanese" eggplants also known as *brinjals*. You can make this dish less spicy by using fewer chilies and more tomatoes in the belado sauce.

1 lb. Japanese eggplant, sliced
1/2 Tbs. salt
2 cups oil (for deep frying)
1 cup sambal belado (p. 71)

- Dissolve the salt in 2 cups of warm water. Soak the eggplant for 5 minutes. Drain.

- Heat the oil and deep fry the eggplant for 3 minutes.

- In a clean wok, sauté the eggplant with the belado sauce for 5 minutes.

- Place on a serving tray with the remainder of the sauce poured over the top.

Vegetables

The Secret of Tofu

Some may complain that the curd of the soybean is bland. But consider that this very blandness is an empty canvas capable of hosting an enormous range of flavors and textures. Tofu was introduced into Indonesia by the Chinese and today it is made in thousands of cottage workshops across the archipelago. It contains the eight essential amino acid required for a complete protein and, like all vegetables, has zero cholesterol.

Pressing. Most Indonesian *tahu* would be considered of a "firm" grade. Softer tofus can be coerced into firmness by pressing the excess water out. Cut slabs of tofu 1-inch thick and wrap them in a clean dry towel. Put a couple of books on top for weight and press for 20 minutes.

Secret. Freeze tofu before you marinate or bake it. It will develop little cracks and fissures and when it thaws out it will soak up your marinades like a sponge resulting in a denser and more textured quality.

TAHU DAN TEMPE GORENG
Deep Fried Tofu and Tempeh

A popular snack that is available in most warungs. Both tahu and tempeh are nutritious not to mention delicious when dipped in hot sambal.

2 cloves garlic
2 shallots
1/2 lb. tempeh, 1/2-inch by 2-inch strips
1 lb. firm tofu, 1 inch squares
2 cups oil (for deep frying)

- Grind the garlic and shallot into a paste and mix with 2 cups water.

- Marinate the tofu and tempeh in this for at least 20 minutes.

- Heat the oil in a wok or deep fryer. Use a strainer or tongs and allow any marinade to drain off the tofu and tempeh before submerging in the oil. Fry until golden brown. (about 5 - 7 minutes).

- Carefully remove from oil and allow to drain on paper towels.

TEMPE KERING
Sweet Dry-Fried Tempeh

Crunchy, sweet, hot, and habit-forming.

1 lb. tempeh, 1/4-inch strips
2 cups oil (for deep-frying)
Bumbu:
  1 Tbs. grated laos (galingale)
  2 clove garlic
  2 shallots
  1 pinch *terasi* (shrimp paste)
1 Tbs. oil (for sauté)
1/2 cup roasted peanuts
4 red chili peppers
1/4 cup tamarind water
2 Tbs. palm sugar
1 pinch salt

- Deep fry tempeh just as with tempe goreng, however cut into smaller pieces and fry until crunchy. Set aside.

- Grind the bumbu and sauté for several minutes in the oil.

- Add the tempeh, and peanuts. Stir-fry for 5 minutes.

- Add the tamarind water and palm sugar. Lower heat and stir until all of the liquid is absorbed. Add salt to taste.

The Secret of Tempeh

Long ago a mound of freshly cooked soybeans was inadvertently mixed with some moldy hibiscus leaves. After incubating for several days at ideal tropical temperatures, the entire lot had fermented into a single cake. In the process enzymes went to work breaking down complex amino acids and rendering tempeh's protein bio-availability higher than chicken.

Tempeh is an extremely cheap and nutritious food often promoted as a solution to world hunger. Its complex nutty flavor (with just a hint of smokey mushrooms) is like a fine cheese whose rewards a worth the effort of acquiring. *Oncom* is a budget relative of tempeh made with soybeans after they have been milked for tofu.

You should be able to find tempeh fresh in healthfood stores or frozen in Asian markets. If you have the inclination, the Internet is a good resource for making your own tempeh.

TAHU SAYUR

Tofu Curry

Tofu is the curry chameleon.

Bumbu:
   1 tsp. coriander seeds, roasted
   4 candlenuts
   1 Tbs. grated laos (galingale)
   1 Tbs. grated turmeric
   1 inch lemon grass, minced
   1/2 tsp. *terasi* (shrimp paste)
1 Tbs. oil (for sauté)
2 lb. deep-fried tofu, 1/2-inch
   cubes
1 cup coconut milk
1 kaffir lime leaf
1 daun salam leaf
1 stalk lemon grass, bruised
1 Tbs. sugar
1 pinch salt and pepper

- Grind the spice bumbu and sauté in oil for 2 minutes.

- Add the remaining ingredients and simmer for 30 minutes.

TEMPE GORENG BUNCIS

Green Beans with Tempeh

1/2 lb. tempeh, 1/4-inch strips
2 cups oil (for deep frying)
Bumbu:
   2 cloves garlic
   2 shallots
   3 hot red chilies
   1 pinch terasi (shrimp paste)
1 Tbs. oil (for sauté)
1/4 lb. green beans, diagonal cut
2 Tbs. sweet soy sauce
1 Tbs. palm sugar
2 Tbs. tomato ketchup

- Deep fry tempeh just as with *tempe goreng* , however cut into smaller strips that will become crunchy when fried. Set aside.

- Grind the bumbu and sauté in the oil for 2 minutes.

- Add the beans and tempeh and stir-fry for another 5 minutes.

- Add 1/2 cup water, sweet soy sauce, palm sugar and ketchup. Lower the heat and cover, allowing it to steam like this for 5 minutes before serving.

SAYUR PEPEYA

Stir-fried Papaya Leaves

Popular with the Sundanese in West Java where they like things a little on the *pahit* (bitter) side.

2 cloves garlic, diced
2 shallots, diced
1/2 tomato, sliced
1/2 Tbs. oil (for sauté)
2 cups papaya leaves
6 red chili peppers, julianned
1/2 Tbs. sugar
1/2 Tbs. sesame oil

- Wash the papaya leaves and cover them with boiling water. Let them steep for a few minutes before draining.

- Sauté the garlic, shallots and tomato in the oil for 2 minutes.

- Add the papaya leaves and Stir-fry for a few minutes.

- Add the remaining ingredients. Stir-fry for about 5 minutes.

SAYUR TAHU PEDAS

Spicy Tofu

As originally prepared, this dish featured a reckless quantity of red and green hot chilies. The less foolhardy can remove the seeds from the chilies or try substituting a few bell peppers.

1 lb. firm tofu, 1/2 inch squares
2 Tbs. lime or lemon juice
4 Tbs. sweet soy sauce
1 tsp. salt
Bumbu:
   1 inch lemon grass
   1 clove garlic
   2 shallots
   1 pinch *terasi* (shrimp paste)
1 Tbs. oil
10 chili peppers, sliced

- Marinate the tofu in the lemon juice, sweet soy sauce, and salt.

- Grind the spice bumbu and sauté for 2 minutes in the oil.

- Add the tofu and stir-fry for 3 minutes.

- Add the chili peppers and stir-fry 5 minutes longer.

- Serve with white rice.

Vegetables

Daging
Meat

With more miles of coastline than any other country, you would expect Indonesians to eat a lot of fresh seafood, but even more common than the saltwater varieties are the freshwater fish and shrimp grown by rice farmers in their flooded padi. *Lele* (catfish) is a favorite that is cheap, easy to bone and, like most of the fish served in warungs, it's usually deep fried. The second most popular cooking method for fish is *bakar* (barbecue). When cooking a fish bakar, a hinged, cage-like grill is often used to keep the fish from falling apart. Look for something similar in your local Asian market.

Other delicacies from the padi include *belut* (eel), *snookie* (snake), and *kodok* (frogs). Where there is water there are also *bebek* (ducks), which are highly regarded for their rich greasy flesh and extra-large eggs. Nearby *ayam kampung* (literally village chicken) run themselves ragged avoiding motorcycles, trucks and small children. Consequently they tend to be a bit leaner and chewier, not to mention tastier than their hormone-fed relatives in the West. Like many traditional dishes, *ayam goreng* (fried chicken) is best eaten with rice, hot *sambal*, and your fingers.

Indonesians traditionally see larger animals as vessels of *semangat,* the sentient force that permeates all life. Sacrificial ceremonies are still practiced, especially in more remote areas where meat is thought to be an agent of fertility and strength. During the Idul Adha holiday, Moslems will often slaughter *kambing* (mutton) and give the meat to the poor.

When ordering kambing dishes you're more likely to get goat than lamb, but it is quite tasty nontheless. Kambing is a favorite meat for *sate* (barbecued kebab skewers) as well.

Many restaurants inform patrons that no pork or pork by-products are used by placing the word *halal* in their windows. However *Babi* (pork) can be found in Chinese restaurants as well as in non-Moslem areas such as Bali, Flores and parts of Sumatra. The Balinese are especially fond of pork and even use the pig's blood to flavor many otherwise vegetarian dishes.

Sapi (cow) is enjoyed all across the archipelago including on Bali where the local Hindus have no taboos against eating beef. Apart from the usual cuts, the beef's skin is quite popular most notably with *nasi gudeg* (p. 91).

SATE

Surprisingly sate is one of the most portable of street foods. The entire rig, complete with a barbecue full of hot coals and all the fixings is carried or rolled from one house to the next. You will find everything from quail eggs to rabbit and even fish heads on a sate skewer, but the most common meats are chicken and mutton.

Sate makes a good fast food because the skewers can be prepared in advance and cooked quickly over a flame made hot with the fanning of a bamboo *kipas*. Little bits of pure fat are often skewered between the meat to contribute their drippings and tease the flames.

The secret to cooking sate is to use a hot flame and turn the skewers often with an occasional dipping into the marinade. If you don't have access to a grill you can broil sate in an oven but you should still turn and dip it often. Obviously the smaller you cut the meat the faster the sate will cook and some street fast-food sate is micro sized.

If preparing sate for a large group seems labor intensive, just marinate the meat overnight and invite your friends to participate in a ritual skewering. With practice you should be able to skewer three or four sticks a minute.

Sate is good with most meats and many vegetables. Try it with shrimp, lobster, eggplant, green pepper, tempeh, or any combination of the above. It is traditionally served with either white rice or *lontong* (p. 82) and covered with a variety of bumbus. A basic peanut-based bumbu that can be made quickly with peanut butter is as follows:

Jyogyanese woman with complete sate rig including barbecue and condiments

2 cloves garlic
2 chili peppers
1 cup natural crunchy peanut butter
1/2 cup coconut milk
3 Tbs. sweet soy sauce
1 pinch salt
1 squeeze lemon juice

• Grind the garlic and chilies and combine in a saucepan with the coconut milk, 1/2 cup of water, and sweet soy sauce. Simmer for 10 minutes. Add salt and lemon juice to taste.

Meats

SATE KAMBING

Pak Wartopo's Mutton Kebabs

This simplified yet equally delicious sate recipe was offered by Pak Wartopo, who balances both sate and red-hot barbecue on either end of a bamboo pole that he plies through the back streets of Malang, East Java.

Bumbu:
    1 Tbs. cumin seeds
    1 chili pepper
    2 cloves garlic
    2 shallots
2 Tbs. sweet soy sauce
1/4 cup tamarind water
1 Tbs. palm sugar
2 lb. boneless mutton, 1/2-inch cubes
15 sate skewers

- Grind the bumbu and mix with the remaining ingredients.

- Marinate the meat for 20 minutes or longer.

- Push about ten pieces of meat on each skewer and grill for 7 minutes turning often.

- The bumbu marinade should be simmered for about 10 minutes. It can then be poured over the sate, or served on the side.

SATE AYAM

Barbecued Chicken Kebabs

This recipe can be used with any meat, but chicken is perhaps the most popular sate in Indonesia.

Bumbu:
    1 tsp. coriander seeds
    1/2 inch ginger
    2 chili peppers
    1 Tbs. palm sugar
1 Tbs. salty soy sauce
1 Tbs. sweet soy sauce
1/2 cup coconut milk
1/4 cup tamarind water
1 tsp. lemon juice
2 lb. boneless chicken, 1/2-inch cubes
15 sate skewers
1/2 cup peanut butter or
    1 cup roasted peanuts, ground

- Grind bumbu and mix with the salty and sweet soy sauces, coconut milk, tamarind water and lemon juice.

- Marinate the chicken for half an hour or longer.

- Push 6-10 chicken morsels onto each bamboo skewer and grill or broil 5 to 10 minutes.

- Meanwhile combine peanuts with the leftover marinade and simmer for 10 minutes.

- Serve the sate skewers over a bed of white rice or lontong with the bumbu on the side, or simply poured over the sate.

SATE LILIT
Balinese Beef Kebabs

Unlike Javanese sate, this meat is first ground and then formed around sugar cane stalks. If you can't find kencur (p. 45), substitute galingale.

Bumbu:
   1 inch lemon grass
   2 clove garlic, peeled
   1 Tbs. grated kencur
   2 chili peppers
2 lb. ground beef
1 cup grated coconut
1 Tbs. palm sugar, crushed
1 pinch salt and pepper
1 Tbs. oil

- Cut 1 inch from the white base of the lemon grass and mince it finely before grinding together with the rest of the bumbu.

- Mix the bumbu and all the remaining ingredients with the ground meat. The oil is to help make the meat stick to the skewers.

- Pat and mold the meat around each skewer so that it is about 5-inches long and 1-inch thick.

- Barbecue the skewers between 5 and 8 minutes. Turn often.

- Serve with rice and hot sambal.

OPOR AYAM BUKITTINGGI

Sumatran Chicken Curry

Wherein the secret of the velvety opor is revealed (picture p. 21).

Bumbu:
- 1 tsp. coriander seeds, roasted
- 4 candlenuts
- 1 Tbs. grated kencur (p. 45)
- 1 Tbs. grated turmeric
- 1 inch lemon grass, minced
- 1 pinch *terasi* (shrimp paste)

2 lb. stewing chicken pieces
1 cup coconut milk
1/4 cup tamarind water
1 kaffir lime leaf
1 daun salam leaf
1 stalk lemon grass, bruised
1 Tbs. sugar
1 pinch salt and pepper

- Grind the spice bumbu.

- Smear the chicken with half the bumbu. Place in a roasting pan and bake at 350 Fahrenheit for 45 min.

- Combine the remaining bumbu in a stock pot with the coconut milk, tamarind water, and cooking leaves. Add the chicken, sugar, salt and pepper.

- Simmer until the sauce thickens (about 1 hour).

AYAM BAKAR

Indonesian Barbecued Chicken

The delicious marinade for this dish works equally well for other meats as well as veggies like eggplant or tempeh.

Bumbu:
- 1 tsp. coriander seeds, roasted
- 4 candlenuts
- 1/2 inch ginger
- 2 cloves garlic
- 2 shallots

1 Tbs. oil
2 lb. chicken pieces
2 Tbs. sweet soy sauce
1 tsp. black pepper

- Grind the spice bumbu and sauté in oil for 2 minutes.

- Stir in 1 cup water and add the chicken. Simmer for 20 minutes before turning off the heat and allowing to marinate.

- Heat your grill. Smear sweet soy sauce on the chicken pieces and pepper them lightly. Grill each piece for about 7 minutes on a side. Reapply marinade and sweet soy sauce as needed.

AYAM GORENG
Indonesian Fried Chicken

Ayam what ayam! (picture p. 20).

Bumbu:
>   1/2 Tbs. coriander seeds
>   2 clove garlic
>   1 Tbs. grated ginger
>   1 Tbs. grated turmeric
>   2 chili peppers
> 1 Tbs. salty soy sauce
> 1/2 cup tamarind water
> 2 lb. frying chicken pieces
> 3 cups oil (for deep frying)

- Grind the spice bumbu paste.

- Combine the chicken in a stock pot with the bumbu, soy sauce, tamarind water, and 2 cups of water. Simmer for about 20 minutes before shutting off the heat and allowing the chicken to marinate (overnight if possible).

- Heat the oil in a wok for deep frying (p. 28). Using tongs briefly drain the marinade from each chicken piece before gently submerging it in the hot oil. Add as much chicken as can float on the surface.

- Fry chicken 12-15 minutes. It will turn golden brown.

- Ayam goreng is usually served with white rice and hot sambal.

AYAM GORENG KELAPA
Coconut Fried Chicken

Coconut milk provides a sensational variation on the deep-fried theme.

Bumbu:
>   1 tsp. coriander seeds, roasted
>   2 candlenuts
>   1/2 inch laos (galingale)
>   1 inch lemon grass, minced
>   1 clove garlic
> 1 Tbs. oil (for sauté)
> 2 lb. frying chicken pieces
> 1 cup coconut milk
> 1 Tbs. sugar
> 1 tsp. salt
> 3 cups oil (for deep frying)

- Grind the bumbu and sauté in the oil for 2 minutes.

- Add the chicken with the coconut milk, sugar, salt, and enough water so the chicken is submerged. Simmer for 10 minutes before shutting off the heat and marinating several hours or overnight.

- Fry as with regular ayam goreng.

Meats

AYAM BELADO
Chicken in Chili-Tomato Sauce

You can make all sorts of dishes with the basic *belado* sauce (p. 71). Try it with hard-boiled eggs, beef, fish, or eggplant. Indonesians deep-fry the meat first, but it can be baked or simply added directly for similar results.

2 lb. chicken pieces
1 cup sambal belado (p. 71)

- Bake or deep fry the chicken for 10 minutes. Alternatively, simply add the chicken raw and cook the belado a little longer.

- Combine the sambal belado with 1 cup of water and the chicken. Simmer over a low heat for 20 minutes. Add more water if necessary.

- Place the chicken on a platter and cover with the remaining belado sauce.

SAMBAL GORENG TELUR
Coconut Fried Eggs

First boiled, then deep-fried, then cooking again in an amazing sauce.

8 eggs, hard-boiled and shelled
Bumbu:
  1 inch lemon grass
  1 Tbs. grated laos (galingale)
  2 shallots
  1 clove garlic
  4 chili peppers
1 stalk lemon grass, bruised
1 medium tomato, diced
1 cup coconut milk
1 Tbs. palm sugar
1 pinch salt
oil (for deep frying and sauté)

- Shell the eggs and deep fry until golden.

- Grind the bumbu and sauté for several minutes before adding the eggs and remaining ingredients. Simmer for 5 minutes.

- Top with the remaining sauce.

ACAR TELUR
Piquant Hard-boiled Eggs

These are best prepared ahead so they have lots of time to marinate.

Bumbu:
- 2 cloves garlic
- 1 Tbs. grated ginger
- 1 inch lemon grass, minced

1 Tbs. oil
1 stalk lemon grass, bruised
6 eggs, hard-boiled and peeled
1/2 cup tamarind water
2 Tbs. vinegar
1 Tbs. salty soy sauce
1 Tbs. sugar

- Grind the bumbu and sauté in the oil for several minutes.

- Add the eggs and all the remaining ingredients with 1/2 cup of water. Simmer for 15 minutes before turning off heat and marinating at least 2 hours.

SEMUR KAMBING
Sweet Cooked Mutton

This dish is traditionally prepared for Idul Fitri, the Islamic holy celebration that occurs at the end of Ramadan

Bumbu:
- 10 pepper corns
- 1/2 tsp. nutmeg
- 3 cloves garlic
- 1 pinch salt

1 Tbs. oil (for sauté)
1 lb. mutton, thinly sliced
2 Tbs. sweet soy sauce
2 tomatoes, sliced
4 red chili peppers, julienned
2 green chili pepper, julienned
1/2 cup fried shallots

- Grind the bumbu and sauté in the oil for a few minutes.

- Add the mutton and brown for 5 minutes.

- Add a cup of water, the sweet soy sauce and tomato. Continue to cook, adding water as necessary, until the meat is tender (about 45 minutes).

- Add the chili peppers and half of the fried shallots. Cook for just a few minutes longer until the red chilies darken.

- Transfer to a serving dish and top with the remainder of the fried shallots.

Meats

GULAI KAMBING

Curried Mutton Stew

This dish manages to incorporate most of the ingredients that made the spice islands famous.

Bumbu:

2 cloves
1/2 tsp. grated nutmeg
1 tsp. cumin seeds, roasted
4 candlenuts
1/2 tsp. terasi (shrimp paste)
1 Tbs. grated ginger
1 Tbs. grated turmeric
2 cloves garlic
2 shallots

1 Tbs. oil
1 lb. mutton, stewing pieces
1/4 cup tamarind water
1 cup coconut milk
1 stick cinnamon
2 kaffir lime leaf
3 chili peppers, chopped

- Grind the bumbu and sauté in the oil for 2 minutes.

- Add the mutton and brown for 5 minutes.

- Add all remaining ingredients and simmer until the liquid thickens (about 45 minutes).

- Serve with white rice.

EMPAL
Dry-Fried Beef

Beef jerky Indonesian style.

1 lb. boneless beef chuck
Bumbu:
  1 Tbs. coriander seeds, roasted
  2 cloves garlic
1 cup coconut milk
1 Tbs. palm sugar
1 tsp. salt
2 cups oil (for deep frying)

• Slice the beef into 1/4-inch thin strips and tenderize.

• Grind the bumbu and sauté in 1 Tbs. of oil for 2 minutes before adding the beef and browning for 5 minutes.

• Add the remaining ingredients and lower the heat. Cook until all of the liquid is absorbed.

• Finally, deep fry the beef until its exterior is crispy.

RENDANG
Beef Roasted Padang Style

Padang restaurants take their name from a city in southern Sumatra where the food is especially rich and hot. The secret to rendang is to slow-cook the meat until it has absorbed virtually all of the coconut milk and spices.

Bumbu:
  4 candlenuts
  1 Tbs. grated ginger
  1 Tbs. grated turmeric
  1 Tbs. grated laos (galingale)
  2 chili peppers
  2 cloves garlic
  2 shallots
1 Tbs. oil
1 lb. stewing beef, 2-inch cubes
1 cup coconut milk
1 stalk lemon grass, bruised
2 salam leaves
1 Tbs. sugar
1 tsp. salt

• Grind the bumbu and sauté in the oil for 2 minutes before adding the beef and browning for 5 minutes.

• Add the remaining ingredients and lower the heat. Simmer gently until most of the liquid is absorbed (up to 3 hours).

RAWON

Beef in Black Pangi Nut Sauce

This dish hails from Semarang, Central Java, where it is often served for breakfast. Westerners will find it more appealing at the dinner hour.

Bumbu:
 1 tsp. coriander seeds, roasted
 2 keluwek nuts (p. 108)
 2 candlenuts
 1 Tbs. grated laos (galingale)
 1 Tbs. grated turmeric
 1 inch lemon grass
 2 shallots
1 Tbs. oil
1 lb. stewing beef, cubed
1 Tbs. salty soy sauce
1/4 cup tamarind water
1 blade lemon grass, bruised

2 chili peppers
1/2 cup bean sprouts

- Grind the bumbu and sauté in the oil for 2 minutes before adding the beef and browning 5 additional minutes.

- Add 2 cups of water and the soy sauce, tamarind water, lemon grass and chili peppers. Simmer for 45 minutes. The rawon should still be quite soupy when finished.

- Garnish with bean sprouts and serve with white rice.

SAMBAL GORENG DAGING

Spicy Fried Beef

Quick and excellent.

Bumbu:
 2 candlenuts
 1 Tbs. grated laos (galingale)
 1 Tbs. grated ginger
 2 cloves garlic
 2 shallots
1 Tbs. oil
1 lb. sirloin, 1/2-inch cubes
3 chili peppers, chopped
1/2 cup coconut milk
1 Tbs. palm sugar

- Grind the bumbu and sauté for 2 minutes before adding the beef and chilies. Stir-fry 5 minutes.

- Add the coconut milk and palm sugar. Simmer for 15 minutes.

- Serve with white rice.

SATE BABI

Barbecued Pork Kebabs

Bumbu:

- 1 tsp. coriander seeds, roasted
- 2 candlenuts
- 1 inch lemon grass
- 1 Tbs. grated ginger
- 2 cloves garlic
- 2 shallots
- 2 chili peppers, chopped

1 Tbs. oil

1 lb. pork, 1/2-inch cubes

2 Tbs. sweet soy sauce

1/2 cup coconut milk

1 Tbs. lime juice

- Grind the bumbu and sauté with the pork. Add remaining ingredients and simmer for 5 minutes. Turn off heat and marinate for 1 hour.

- Skewer and grill about 7 minutes, turning often.

ABON BABI

Balinese Mixed Pork

This is a fantastic way to prepare any cut of pork. It is usually served as part of a nasi rames (assorted small dishes with rice).

1 lb. pork tenderloin.

Bumbu:

- 1 tsp. whole pepper corns
- 1 inch lemon grass, minced
- 1/2 Tbs. grated turmeric
- 1/2 Tbs. grated kencur (p. 45)
- 2 clove garlic
- 2 shallots
- 1/2 tsp. grated nutmeg
- 2 red chili peppers
- 1/2 tsp. *terasi* (shrimp paste)

1 Tbs. oil (for sauté)

1 small tomato, sliced

1 leaf salam

1 pinch salt

- Boil or bake pork until done.

- Grind the spice bumbu and shred the pork. Mix together, working the bumbu into the meat with your fingers.

- Stir-fry the pork for 10 minutes before adding the remaining ingredients. Cook until tender (about 30 minutes).

- Garnish w/ slices of red chili.

Meats

KARE IKAN
Sumatran Fish Curry

Bumbu:

    1 tsp. coriander seeds, roasted
    1 inch lemon grass
    1 Tbs. grated ginger
    1 Tbs. grated turmeric
    2 cloves garlic
    2 shallots
2 lb. white fish
1 stalk lemon grass, bruised
1/2 cup coconut milk
2 tsp. soy sauce

1 Tbs. palm sugar
2 chili peppers, chopped
1 salam leaf

- Grind the bumbu and mix with 1/2-cup water. Marinate the fish in this for 20 minutes.

- Remove the fish and heat the marinade in a wok together with the remaining ingredients. Simmer for 5 minutes.

- Add the fish to the sauce and cover. Simmer lightly until the fish is done. Depending on the thickness of the fish, you may or may not have to turn it.

- Place the fish on a serving dish and pour the sauce over the top. You can garnish it with a little chopped red chili, lemon, and *kamanggi* (lemon basil). Serve with white rice.

PEPES IKAN

Fish Grilled in a Banana Leaf

This fish gives great texture due to a bumbu of finely chopped seasonings.

Bumbu:

    1/2 cup chopped coconut

    2 chili pepper, chopped

    2 cloves garlic, minced

    1 inch lemon grass, minced

    2 shallots, minced

    1 Tbs. sweet soy sauce

    1 pinch salt

2 lb. cod

2 banana leaves and toothpicks

1/2 lemon

- Chop all the bumbu ingredients and combine.

- Spread half the bumbu in the center of a banana leaf. Place the fish on top and cover with the remaining bumbu.

- Place another banana leaf on top and roll as shown on page 30. If you are using aluminum foil you won't need toothpicks.

- Depending on the size of the fish grill for about 5 minutes on each side, If baking, cook about 10 minutes at 325 degrees Fahrenheit.

- Serve on the opened leaf with a squeeze of lemon.

PECEL LELE

Javanese Fried Catfish

This basic marinade is used for many types of deep-fried fish.

2 cloves garlic

1 Tbs. lemon juice

2 lb. catfish

2 cups oil (for deep frying)

1/4 cup sambal tomat (p. 69)

1/2 cup *kamanggi* (lemon basil)

1 cucumber, sliced

- Grind the garlic into a paste and mix with 1 cup water and lemon juice. Marinate the fish in this for 15 minutes. Drain.

- Heat the oil in a wok. Fry catfish until golden brown.

- Serve with sambal, kamanggi and cucumber (the *pecel*).

GURAMI BAKAR
Sweet Grilled Fish

Gurami fish swim in flooded rice paddies and taste a bit like trout.

Bumbu:
    4 candlenuts
    1/2 Tbs. grated turmeric
    2 cloves garlic
    2 shallots
1 Tbs. oil
2 lb. gurami, trout, or steelhead
2 Tbs. sweet soy sauce
1 tsp. black pepper

- Grind the spice bumbu and sauté in the oil for 2 minutes.

- Stir in 1 cup water and add the fish. Turn off the heat and marinate for 20 minutes .

- Heat your grill. Smear sweet soy sauce over the fish and pepper lightly. Depending on the size of the fish, grill for around 3 minutes on a side.

UDANG GORENG
Fried Shrimp

Most Indonesians eat shrimp with the shell, which adds a nice crunchiness.

2 cloves garlic, mashed
1 Tbs. lemon juice
1 tsp. salt
1 tsp. pepper
1 lb. shrimp
2 cups oil (for deep frying)
1/2 cup all-purpose flour
2 Tbs. butter
1 clove garlic, minced
1/2 cup *kamanggi* (lemon basil)
1 cucumber, sliced

- Combine the garlic with 1 cup water, lemon juice, salt, and pepper. Marinate the shrimp in this for 15 minutes.

- Heat the oil in a wok. Remove the shrimp from the marinade and dip them briefly in the flour before frying briefly. The cooking time will depend on the size of the shrimp.

- In a clean wok, melt the butter and sauté the minced garlic for a minute.

- Add the prawns and sauté just 30 seconds to warm them up.

- Serve with lemon basil and cucumber.

SAMBAL GORENG UDANG

Shrimp Cooked in Coconut Milk

The sambal goreng is one of the finer achievements of Indonesian cuisine.

Bumbu:

- 1 inch lemon grass stalk
- 3 candlenuts
- 1 Tbs. grated laos (galingale)
- 2 cloves garlic
- 2 shallots
- 3 chili peppers
- 1 pinch *terasi* (shrimp paste)

- 1 Tbs. oil
- 1/4 lb. snow peas, trimmed
- 1/2 lb. shrimp
- 2 Tbs. tamarind water
- 1/2 cup coconut milk
- 1 Tbs. palm sugar
- 1 pinch salt

- Grind the bumbu and sauté for 2 minutes before adding the snow peas. Stir-fry 2 minutes.

- Add the prawns and stir-fry briefly for 1 minute before adding the remaining ingredients. Simmer for a few minutes so that the prawns are pink yet the snow peas are still crisp.

Makanan Penutup
Sweet Snacks

Indonesians don't really think in terms of dessert. If anything they might simply crave a little fresh fruit and some tea or coffee after a meal. But don't let that stop you from experimenting with desserts as the chemistry between coconut milk, palm sugar, and the pandan leaf is definitely worth exploring.

top: steamed sticky rice cakes and dipping sauce

right: assorted kue

below: jenang and jadah in Bandung, Java

In the mornings you might be greeted by the kue lady peddling her baked, boiled, fried or steamed little cakes and pastries from door to door. A little like Indonesian dim sum, you never know what scrumptious goodies might lie wrapped up inside those banana leaves. Around noon when the heat is taking over, the *"es"* vendors come out with icy sundaes of all kinds. As things cool down in the afternoons little fried delicacies like *pisang goreng* (fried bananas) make the rounds. Later after you've had a chance to digest your dinner, you can try a giant chocolate-stuffed *martabak*.

As usual, Indonesians love to contrast flavors. Whether it be pouring a little salted coconut milk over some sweet black rice pudding, or serving some fiery bird peppers with sweet-fried tempeh, there is always a surprise in store. Hot candied ginger makes a regular appearance in sweet soups that are served warm, and shocking combinations of fruit and gelatinous candied confections are mixed with wild abandon in icy treats that blur the line between a dessert and a beverage (see *es teler*, p. 55).

Some of these sundaes are served in a glass with a straw, and others in a bowl with a spoon. The basic theme is to start with a mountain of shaved ice and proceed to adorn it with everything from tart tropical fruits, to brightly colored pearls of sago palm jelly, cubes of jellied agar agar, and bits of fermented sticky rice. The entire affair is then topped with rose syrup and a dollop of sweetened condensed milk. It may sound disgusting, but if done right it's more refreshing than ice cream.

SANGREN ULEK

Sticky Rice Bars

Salty and sweet.

1 cup white sticky rice
1 cup serundeng (p. 68)
1/2 cup palm sugar

- Soak the sticky rice in water for several hours or overnight.

- Combine with 2 cups of water and cook at a gentle simmer for about 45 minutes. Add more water if it becomes too dry.

- Allow the rice to cool for 10 minutes before pouring it out onto a clean surface or some wax paper. The pudding-like rice should ooze out and form a blob about 1-inch thick. Cut the blob into 2-inch squares.

- Pour the serundeng into a bowl or plate and mix in the sugar. Dip and roll each rice bar until thoroughly coated.

ES CAMPUR

Mixed Up Shaved Ice

Ice that is properly shaved is like snow; it melts in your mouth without lots of big chunks to give you a headache. Little hand-cranked machines imported from China do the job nicely, or just use crushed ice. Add chocolate to your sweetened condensed milk for an extra kick and use any fruits that sound good to you.

1 avocado
1 mango
1 papaya
1/2 cup coconut milk
1 pinch salt
1/4 cup palm sugar
shaved or crushed ice
1/2 cup sweet condensed milk

- Cut the fruits into bite-sized pieces.

- Heat the coconut milk with a little salt, but don't let it curdle. Dissolve in the palm sugar and allow it to cool.

- Shave a nice snowball of ice into each bowl.

- Pile some pieces of fruit on the ice and cover with the coconut milk and sweetened condensed milk.

KUE WAJIK

Sticky Rice Triangles

1 cup white sticky rice
1 cup coconut milk
1 cup palm sugar
1 tsp. vanilla extract
1/2 tsp. salt

- Soak the rice in water for several hours or overnight.

- Rinse and combine rice with 1 cup of water, coconut milk, palm sugar, vanilla, and salt.

- Simmer for 45 minutes. The rice should bubble like a pudding; add more water if it becomes too dry.

- Allow the rice to cool for 10 minutes before pouring it out onto a clean surface. The pudding-like rice should ooze out and form a blob about 1-inch thick. Cut into triangles about 3 inches on a side.

- Allow to cool until the triangles are fully set.

TAHU DAN TEMPE BACIM

Sweet Tofu and Tempeh

This sweet and nutritious snack is often eaten with fiery bird peppers.

1 cup palm sugar
1 lb. tofu
1 lb. tempeh
2 salam leaves
1 Tbs. grated laos (galingale)
1 tsp. salt
2 cups oil (for deep-frying)
12 bird peppers (just for fun)

- Heat 4 cups water in a stockpot and dissolve in the palm sugar.

- Grind the laos root and combine in the stockpot with the tofu, tempeh and salam leaves. Cook until most of the liquid has been absorbed.

- For authenticity deep-fry the tofu and tempeh for about 4 minutes. Alternatively you can slow-bake them in an oven at 250 degrees for about 1 hour.

JADAH
Sticky Rice Loafs

It takes a little time to make these luminous oval treats, but if you like sticky rice it's well worth the effort. Jadah needs to be cooked for a long time so that the rice can lose its grain and become a solid mass.

1 cup white sticky rice
1 cup coconut milk
1/2 tsp. salt

- Soak the rice in water for several hours or overnight.

- Rinse and combine rice with 1 cup of water, the coconut milk, and salt. Cook at a gentle simmer for about 2 hours. Add more water if it becomes too dry.

- Allow the jadah to cool for 10 minutes before pouring it out onto some wax paper.

- When the rice is cool enough to be handled, make little paddies about 1-inch wide by 2 inches long. Allow to set for 30 minutes or so.

Sweet Snacks

BUBUR KACANG HIJAU

Balinese Mung Bean Porridge

This porridge even makes mung beans taste good.

1/2 cup white sticky rice
1 cup mung beans
1/2 cup palm sugar
1 plantain, sliced
1 cup coconut milk
1 pinch salt

- Soak the rice and mung beans in water for several hours.

- Rinse and cook in 4 cups of water for about 30 minutes.

- Add the remaining ingredients and salt to taste.

BUBUR KETAN HITAM

Sweet Black Rice Porridge

This sweet rice dessert is offered in Wonosobo, a hill town in central Java where the evenings might almost be considered chilly.

1 cup black sticky rice, soaked
1/4 cup palm sugar
1/2 tsp. salt
1/2 cup thick coconut milk

- Soak the rice in water for several hours or overnight.

- Drain rice and combine with 2 cups water in a pan. Heat to a boil before reducing heat and simmering covered for 1 hour.

- Add more water if necessary to keep the porridge runny.

- Dissolve in the palm sugar and shut off the heat. The rice should congeal a little to the thickness of a nice pudding.

- In a separate pan, heat the coconut milk and dissolve in the salt.

- Serve in bowls with a dollop of the salted coconut milk on top.

PISANG GORENG

Tias' Fried Bananas

You can use plantains or slightly green bananas. This is magic with a scoop of ice cream.

1/2 cup rice flour
1 pinch salt
1/2 cup coconut milk
1 tsp. vanilla
1 egg
4 ripe plantains, quartered
oil (for deep frying)

• Mix the rice flour with the salt. Slowly mix in the coconut milk, avoiding lumps. Add the vanilla and beat in the egg.

• Heat the oil in a wok.

• Dip the banana quarters in batter and fry until golden.

KUE SERABI

Green Pandan Crepes

A favorite snack in Jakarta, where vendors crank out scores of the delicate crepes from a bank of 4 tiny woks. The secret here is to let the batter sit undisturbed for 2 hours allowing a mild fermentation to occur.

1 cups rice flour
1 Tbs. baking powder
1 cup coconut milk
2 pandan leaves
**   or 2 drops pandan extract**
1/4 cup palm sugar
1/2 Tbs. oil

• Mix the flour, baking powder and coconut milk with enough water to make a runny batter.

• Add the sugar and pandan. Allow to ferment for 2 hours.

• Lightly oil and heat a wok to a moderate temperature. Ladle in enough batter to create one thin 6-inch crepe in the center.

• Cook slowly for about two minutes on one side only . The center should puff up and the edges become crispy.

Epilog
The Cult of Martabak

March 23, 2002, Bandung
After questing across this archipelago in search of some trace of the elusive and timeless secret of the *opor*, I have found myself hopelessly sidetracked by a strange and alarming cult. Every evening it begins the same with people gathering around the *Kue Bandung* stalls, waiting for the magic to begin. Here in Bandung they are known simply as *martabak*, and it is here that I have come to the very edge of what constitutes rational cuisine.

Martabak like this are generally only available in the evenings, probably because eating something this rich during the heat of the day would prove fatal. Like a good pizza joint, the best warungs don't sell display models but make each martabak to order. The chef's performance alone is worth the price of the martabak, which weighing in at over a kilo of flour, chocolate, butter, cheese, and sweetened condensed milk does not come cheap by Indonesian standards.

On balance, the martabak doesn't contain all that much more fat and sugar then your average "death by chocolate" Western cake. And because all the evil stuff is added last, while still in its raw state, you really get all the possible mileage out of the sin. Still, when you watch the *tukang martabak* at work, you might cringe at the excessive, gratuitous, even hedonic abandon with which he applies each successive topping.

The batter is similar to a Western pancake, but the martabak is cooked on one side only so that the top is bubbly and ready for butter, lots of butter. After lathering it up and letting nearly a cup of butter soak deep into the pores, a quarter of a can or so of sweetened condensed milk is poured on. For fillings you can select among peanuts, cheese, and chocolate sprinkles; those *püür chocoladevlokken* sprinkles that Dutch and Indonesian folks like to cover their toast with in the morning. I used to stop short of the cheddar cheese, but once I realized how strangely wonderful it is in combination with butter and chocolate I was hooked. Add another light coat of sweetened condensed milk and the martabak is ready to be folded and buttered again, this time with a special butter that is 100% *murni* (pure).

It is here that I must withdraw and attempt to digest this cacophony of culinary practices thus far encountered. My mind is as full as my stomach and I have become obsessed with defining something that cannot be quantified. In the end I am left with some pretty good recipes, and the dream of returning again someday to begin the search anew.

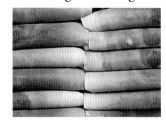

MARTABAK MANIS

Sinfully Stuffed Giant Pancake

1 tsp. baker's yeast

2 cup all-purpose wheat flour

2 medium eggs

1/4 tsp. baking soda

1/2 cup butter

1/2 cup sweet-condensed milk

Toppings of your choice:

   1/2 cup chopped peanuts

   1/2 cup chocolate sprinkles

   1/2 lb. cheddar or jack cheese

- Heat 1 cup of water in a pan or in the microwave until it is warm but not too hot to touch. Mix in the yeast and allow it to sit in a warm place for 15 minutes.

- Mix the flour with the baking soda. Add the yeasted water and mix well. Beat in the eggs. Aim for a batter that is thick, but will still pour easily. Thin with water if necessary.

- Leave the batter to cure undisturbed for 15 minutes.

- Heat and butter a griddle lightly. Pour enough batter in to completely cover the bottom and roll the pan around to spread the batter 1 inch up the sides of the pan. The center of the martabak should be about 1/2-inch thick.

- Cover and cook at a medium heat for about 10 minutes or until the top is bubbly but firm and the bottom golden brown.

- Remove the martabak and place on a counter top. Butter the top liberally. Adorn with the sweetened condensed milk and the toppings of your choice.

- Fold the martabak in half like an omelet and butter the top. Serve warm.

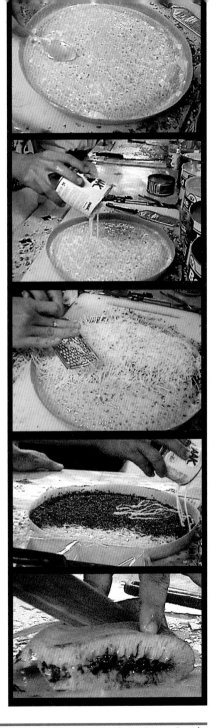

Pronunciation Guide

Bahasa Indonesia is the National language of the Republic of Indonesia. It possesses a remarkably flexible grammar that is easy to read and pronounce. There are no tenses in Indonesian and plurality is often indicated by a simple doubling of the word. The most common sounds are included below as a brief guide.

Single vowels are pronounced roughly the same as English soft vowels, for example *a* as in *bar*, and *o* as in *nob*.

Double vowels are pronounced as two syllables, that is with a slight pause between the sounds.

When *b* comes at the beginning of a word it is pronounced like the English *b*, but as a final letter it is pronounced like an English *p*

The letter *c* is always pronounced like the *ch* in chair.

An *r* that does not begin a word is trilled like a Spanish *r*.

Good morning / day / afternoon / evening
Selemat pagi / siang / sore / malam

What's up (what's the news)?
Apa Kabar?

Where do you want to go?
Mau ke mana?

What are you looking for?
Dari apa?

What do you call this?
Apa ini?

How much is this?
Berapa harganya?

Expensive!
Mahal!

Can it be cheaper?
Bisa kurang?

I want it with no MSG!
Saya mau ini tanpa aji no moto

I want it not too sweet.
Sedikit manis saja

I want it with no sugar.
Mau ini tanpa gula

Can I take it to go?
Mau ini bungkus

This is delicious!
Enak sekali!

Fried
Goreng

Stir-fried
Tumis

Grilled
Bakar

Enjoy your meal.
Selemat makan.

Index

Conversions:

Convert Fahrenheit to Celsius
(Fahrenheit - 32) * (5 / 9)

1 oz. (ounce)
28.3495 grams

1 lb. (pound)
16 oz = 453.59 grams = 0.45359 kilo

100 grams
3.527 oz

1 kg (kilogram)
2.2046 lb.

1 Tbs. (tablespoon)
15 ml. (milliliter)

1 tsp. (teaspoon)
5 ml. (milliliter)

1 fluid oz.
2 Tbs. = 29.57 ml.

1 cup
16 Tbs. = 8 fl. oz = 236 ml.

1 quart
0.946 liters

1 gallon
0.833 Imperial Gallons, = 3.785 liters

1 liter
1.06 quarts = 4.237 cups = 33.8 fl. oz.